Wild Open Spaces

For the Appeli's,
The spirit of the Wild West
lives on in all of us.

[signature]

WILD OPEN SPACES

WHY WE LOVE WESTERNS

Yardena Rand

MANVILLE, RI

Printed in the United States of America
Jacket and text design by Bookwrights
Jacket painting, *Lone Rider* © Thom Ross, used with permission
Stills courtesy of Photofest (212-633-6330) and The Roy Rogers-Dale Evans Museum; historical photos courtesy of the Buffalo Bill Historical Center, Harry Rinker and U.S. Television Office, Inc., and Harvard College Library. Line art courtesy of Dover.

Publisher's Cataloging-in-Publication
(Provided by Quality Books, Inc.)

Rand, Yardena.
    Wild open spaces : why we love Westerns / Yardena
Rand.
        p. cm.
        Includes bibliographical references and index.
        ISBN 1-932991-44-1

        1. Western films--United States--History and
criticism.   I. Title.

    PN1995.9.W4R36 2005   791.43'6278
                                  QBI04-200370

Library of Congress Control Number: 2004113539

Published by
Maverick Spirit Press
P.O. Box 113
Manville, RI 02838
401.405.0178
sales@maverickspiritpress.com
www.maverickspiritpress.com

To Western fans everywhere

ONTENTS

ACKNOWLEDGMENTS

John Wayne as Captain Nathan Brittles, *She Wore a Yellow Ribbon* (1949), courtesy Photofest

Wild Open Spaces was originally written as my doctoral dissertation (and has since been completely overhauled, don't worry!). But when I was in graduate school, I had a crazy notion that Westerns had a far broader appeal than most people realized. My director and long-time friend, Professor Bruce Rosenberg, shares my love of the West (and the Western) and didn't even flinch when I kept insisting Westerns had a diverse audience and wanted to prove it by interviewing Western fans. I thank him for his support and his example; in his wonderful intellect and unwillingness to give up in the face of great personal hardship, he is an inspiration. I also received invaluable help and guidance from Professor Susan Smulyan. She stood by my rather unorthodox approach and helped shape the interpretation of results into the book you have before you today. I'm lucky she was in my corner. Thanks, Susan.

Of course, deciding to interview Western fans and actually doing it are hardly one and the same. Newspaper editors assisted me in reaching the many Western fans I heard from in the initial phase of this research. I am especially grateful to Dana Cartwright who, at the time, worked for the *San Antonio Express-News*. Her suggestion that I send out a press release announcing word of my research and telling readers how to participate enabled me to survey over 500 Western fans.

The qualitative information I gathered early on from this first set of interviews formed the basis of my dissertation, but I wanted to update that research with a quantitative survey when I decided to write this book (I knew the audience was diverse, but I wanted to be able to profile it more accurately—just how many people *did* love Westerns, and how representative were they of the U.S. population as a whole?). In this phase, I relied on the help and generosity of a telephone survey house I have worked with many times in the past as well as colleagues in the field of statistical analysis. Heartfelt thanks go to Chris Ricci of Ricci Telephone, my good friend and SPSS wizard, Gail Piasecki D'Agostino, and my favorite stats guru, Dr. Rick Pollack.

The photos you will see in this book have been painstakingly selected for the emotions conveyed, specific actions shown, and particular moments captured. I am indebted to the many people who took my emails and listened patiently on the phone as I tried to communicate the nuance of what I was looking for: "I need something with Gary Cooper in *High Noon* showing pain on his face—not anger, but pain"; "have you got something with John Wayne in *The Searchers* expressing both resolve and horror?"; "I'd love to publish a shot of Roy Rogers that my readers, who are avid Western fans, might not have seen before—what have you got?" These folks pulled out files, looked through collections, and described images over the phone to me in such detail I was able to envision them clearly. And along the way they found images that were even better than what I had in mind! My sincere gratitude goes to Ann Marie Donoghue of the Buffalo Bill Historical Center, Holger Wrede of the U.S. Television Office, Dave Koch of The Roy Rogers-Dale Evans Museum, Dave DelVal of moviemarket.com, Jerry Ohlinger of Jerry Ohlinger's Movie Material Store in NYC, and especially Howard Mandelbaum of Photofest. Movie stills are by nature dramatic—they are designed to evoke emotion—I hope you enjoy them!

I have benefited tremendously from colleagues in the writing and publishing fields. They have shared their experiences and given freely of their time and expertise. First, to my Pub-Forum listmates who have conferred, advised, and commiserated—how could I have done this without you?! I especially want to acknowledge Barbara DesChamps, Tordis Isselhardt, Sheri Menelli, Deb Robson, Susan Sabo, and Sue Schrems. Second, I have had the great fortune of befriending Eric Albert, whose exceptional word-smithing talents have greatly improved this book, not to mention given it a dynamite title. Something or someone was smiling on me the day he piped in with "Wild Open Spaces." I can't thank him enough. Finally, I am grateful to have found Mayapriya Long of Bookwrights. She has taken my raw manuscript, photos, and broad ideas and crafted them into a beautifully designed book. May you delight in thumbing through it as much as I do.

Help has also come from other unexpected places. As you will see in the Introduction, the idea for this book germinated in conversations about the movie *Dances with Wolves* I had with several Pawnee in 1991. I am especially grateful to Robert Chapman, Brummett Echohawk, and Ralph Haymond for giving their time and sharing their candid thoughts on this and many other Westerns. I also want to extend my appreciation to artist Thom Ross. In looking for artwork for the cover of this book, I happened on his painting, "Lone Rider." It wasn't close to what I was looking for—it was *exactly* what I was looking for: colorful, angular, full of motion. When I contacted him, having no idea what the licensing fees might be, he graciously granted permission, even supplying the slides I needed for the cover design. When I think of why *I* love Westerns, this painting goes a long way to capturing it for me…and I hope it does for you, too.

Of course, no author can pull a book together without the support of family and friends, and I am no exception. My friend Betsy Herrick lent her graphic design eye to improve logos and graphs. My Cowboy Action Shooting compadres read and commented on the manuscript, in particular Bill English (aka Happy Trails), Heather Kresser (aka Half-a-Hand Henri), and Peter and Joan Carlson (aka One-Ear Pete and Eula Nissen). At the time I wanted to start writing the book, I held a senior position in a small company. My former boss, Kathryn Korostoff, gave me a two month leave-of-absence so I could see if I had the book in me. Each person has made a difference in making this book a reality. Thank you.

I am also lucky to have an extraordinary family. To my parents, for showing me the value of persistence and the importance of pursuing excellence while having a damn good time in life, I thank you. To my grandmother, who still gives 'em hell at age 97, go get 'em "Pete"! And to my darlin' for undying support and love, thank you for making every day of my life a delight.

Finally, to the many fans who gave so generously of their time and really thought through why they love Westerns so much—this book would be nothing without you.

Why Westerns?

*It ain't so much the things we don't know
that get us into trouble. It's the things we
do know that just ain't so.*

Artemus Ward

It started because I wanted to win an argument with
my father. We were talking about a headline-grabbing
new Western, *Dances with Wolves*. My father was emotionally moved by the film—its grandeur, its portrayal of
native cultures, its depiction of the treatment of animals.
He felt the movie captured both the beauty and tragedy of
American frontier history. He just loved it.

Lakota warriors observing from a
ridge, *Dances with Wolves* (1990),
courtesy Photofest

I, by contrast, found many aspects of the movie disturbing (I was in graduate school at the time and highly critical of popular
movies). Yes, I enjoyed the presentation of the Sioux—it was wonderful to see Lakota life portrayed so warmly and completely—but overall
I found the movie simplistic and manipulative. The depictions of white
culture were absurd, I thought, from the incompetent military leadership
to the revolting frontiersmen to the sadistic common soldiers. But mostly
I was completely dismayed by the portrayal of the Pawnee. In his novel
of the same name, Michael Blake, who won an Academy Award for his
screenplay based on the book, describes the Pawnee as:

...the most terrible of all the tribes. The Pawnee saw with unsophisticated but ruthlessly efficient eyes, eyes that, once fixed on an object, decided in a twinkling whether it should live or die. And if it was determined that the object should cease to live, the Pawnee saw to its death with psychotic precision. When it came to dealing death, the Pawnee were automatic, and all of the Plains Indians feared them as they did no one else.

"The most terrible of all the tribes?" All the tribes were terrible, but the Pawnee were the *most* terrible? Unsophisticated? Ruthless?

Wes Studi as "The Toughest" in *Dances with Wolves* (1990), courtesy Photofest

Psychotic? Automatic? As for being feared by all the Plains Indians as they feared "no one else," the Pawnee word for the Sioux, "Tsu-ra-rat," translates as Throat Cutters—the Sioux were known to slit the throats of Pawnee women working in the fields and young men herding horses. Blake's is hardly a friendly, sophisticated, or enlightened description of the Pawnee. And yet his novelistic image was translated without alteration onto Costner's screen.

So when my father exasperatedly fired, "Well, the Sioux love it!" I in my antagonized state countered with, "What's not to love if you're Sioux? But I'll bet the Pawnee hate it!"

And thus was born an idea.

I had a book listing Indian tribal headquarter information around the country—addresses, phone numbers. So I flipped through the index… Pawnee, Pawnee…and there it was: Pawnee, Oklahoma. I figured I would call, talk to a couple of people, and gather all the evidence I needed to make my case—believe me, I knew *exactly* what they would say.

Such are the vagaries of life that a seemingly insignificant decision, made in a moment of arrogance, can have a profound and lasting impact. I called Pawnee, Oklahoma, and was fortunate to speak with the tribal chairman, financial officer, a respected elder, and several others in the office. To a person, they loved the movie. I was dumbfounded. What did they love about it?

First, that Costner used Indian actors and presented the Indian point of view resonated strongly. President of the Pawnee Tribal Council Robert Chapman found the movie:

> …*touching and exciting at times. It showed the Indian point of view and showed Indians were human beings, too.*

Asked if the portrayal of the Pawnee offended him in any way, he replied:

> *No, we were just happy to be mentioned. If it's the Sioux being portrayed, fine. At least they're saying the Indian was human. We can identify with that.*

Pawnee tribal financial officer Ralph Haymond also enjoyed the movie:

The thing that struck me most was the actors are all Indian. It was authentic. Using all Indians is a landmark achievement for all Indians. That's the thing I was most pleased about.

Referring to the movie's popularity throughout the Pawnee community, he also noted people enjoyed seeing the Pawnee portrayed as young and strong and free. Although he felt that historically speaking the Pawnee would have been the ones to accept and adopt Lt. Dunbar (Kevin Costner), he did not ultimately begrudge the movie's perspective:

The way the Sioux portrayed themselves and the Pawnee, it was just the reverse. Put it the other way and it's more realistic. At the same time, I'm very proud of all Indian peoples—they fought and resisted the taking over of their country.

Brummett Echohawk, noted Pawnee actor, painter, writer, veteran, and historian of the Pawnee nation, expressed complete disgust with most Hollywood renditions of Indians. But he was pleased with what he felt was an accurate portrayal in *Dances with Wolves*. He was glad Costner

Rodney A. Grant as Wind in His Hair, *Dances with Wolves* (1990), courtesy Photofest

used "real Indian people and there were no headbands in sight," a practice started early on in the film industry to keep white actors' black wigs from flying off during chase scenes. He noted the discussion among the warriors before "The Toughest" attacked and killed muleskinner Timmons was true to what would have occurred. That the warriors were allowed to make their own decisions and act on their own judgments indicated to Echohawk some care had been taken to do justice to Pawnee social and cultural interactions.

Himself the grandson of a Pawnee scout who served in Major Frank North's all-Pawnee battalion in the 1860s and a decorated veteran of World War II, Echohawk spoke at length about the Pawnee warrior tradition. For him, *Dances with Wolves* was meaningful because:

…it made the point we were very powerful. You could hardly call this tribe a weak-kneed bunch.

Thinking of the film brought back memories of his experiences during World War II. Late in the war, he recalled, his all-Indian brigade from Oklahoma, along with a white brigade from Texas, led a beach assault against the Germans in Italy. When the battle was over, he was sent to sketch portraits of German prisoners-of-war. He found out through translators the Germans had been absolutely terrified before the battle because they had heard in advance they would be fighting not only cowboys, but Indians, too.

We weren't pussy-footing around. We were fighting men.

For Echohawk, *Dances with Wolves* evoked a strong warrior tradition, a tradition he shared, took pride in, and carried on.

This is not to say, of course, all Pawnee—or all Sioux, for that matter—related to and loved *Dances with Wolves*. When I described my conversations to a Pawnee graduate student at the University of California at Los Angeles, for example, he was dismayed, exclaiming, "What's hap-

Remington artwork, courtesy Dover

pened to our people that they would like such a movie?" But it is to say people have many reasons for their preferences, dictated by personal experiences, distinctive histories, cultural backgrounds—all kinds of things we cannot possibly know…unless we ask.

This series of conversations with the Pawnee changed me both personally and professionally. In 1990, I was a scholar in training at an Ivy League university, specializing in twentieth-century American culture with a particular interest in popular culture. Absorbing the latest in cultural theory, I was adamant movies *imposed* ways of thinking on the society at large, *setting* social relationships, *dictating* proper modes of behavior. Most movies, Westerns in particular, I believed, promoted a narrow point of view, privileging white men at the expense of women and people of color, and rewriting history to gloss over the bad faith, cruelty, and exploitation that characterized much of that era.

But what I failed to realize was people have a peculiar ability to approach movies (and other forms of popular culture, not to mention history) from their own perspectives and find value in many unexpected ways. Take, for example, Dolly Stanley-Roberson, a Navajo woman, niece to the three Stanley brothers John Ford featured prominently in the Westerns he filmed in Monument Valley. She tells the story that when *The Searchers* (1956) was shown on the reservation in 1959, people traveled for miles, filling the Chapter House to see the film. As she recalled to an interviewer:

> *The Searchers* is really a very serious film and everyone was quiet until the Indian parts began. Then it was like watching home movies. Everyone would laugh and call out names of who they saw on the screen. The whole movie became more like the funniest comedy ever filmed.

Even viewing *Stagecoach* 40 years after it was filmed was a moving experience for her:

> I recognized each one of my uncles and several others as well. It seemed strange to see them when they were all such young men because I knew them only when they were older. For me, it was almost like watching a part of Navajo history.

Certainly this is a unique circumstance—not many people are related to the Stanley brothers who appeared in John Ford's Westerns.
But what all these examples suggested to me was people could interpret
movies I considered to be narrow and manipulative in meaningful and
empowering ways (my goodness, know their own minds?). Even more,
they indicated to me, whereas Westerns could certainly be seen as prob-

Clockwise from top left, Michael Landon, Pernell Roberts, Lorne Greene, Dan Blocker, *Bonanza* (c. 1963), courtesy Photofest

lematic, there was a lot more going on. I had to acknowledge, despite my "knowing better," people, especially people I wouldn't expect to enjoy them, could find a great deal of personal significance in many Westerns. In fact, if I were honest, I had to admit I'd linger on a good old-fashioned Western myself if I were flipping through channels late at night and came across one (I could never pass up *True Grit* or *The Magnificent Seven*).

Truth be told, like most baby boomers, I grew up on Westerns. My mother, having grown up reading Zane Grey novels, didn't miss an episode of *Rawhide* or *Bonanza* if she could help it and she passed that love of the genre on to me. As a child in the 1960s, I eagerly anticipated weekly installments that kept me up-to-date on the goings-on at the Ponderosa, the Barkley ranch, the High Chaparral, and in Dodge City. I'd join the Cartwright boys on my imaginary pinto, the wind rushing through my hair as I galloped across meadows teaming with high grasses, picking my feet carefully as I negotiated dangerous mountain trails, all to foil dastardly plots that would have succeeded but for my eleventh-hour heroic intervention.

When I was a teenager, my mother and I toured the United States on a motorcycle and we lingered as long as we possibly could in our favorite regions—the West and Southwest. We experienced the grandeur of some of the nation's most spectacular national parks—Yellowstone, Grand Tetons, Bryce, Zion, Grand Canyon, Arches, Capitol Reef. We camped in groves of quaking aspen and ponderosa pine, by gleaming rivers, and in quiet meadows. We explored historic cowboy camps, visited Monument Valley and Canyon de Chelly, stood on the Four Corners, and feasted on Navajo fry bread. We were even chased by buffalo in Custer State Park, South Dakota.

My love of the West and the Western runs deep.

So when I had concluded my conversations with the Pawnee, two burning questions remained: If they could find meaning in *Dances with Wolves*, what did a wide variety of people think about Westerns? What other viewpoints were out there?

And that is the genesis of the book you have before you. In 1994, I conducted a national survey, interviewing 552 Western fans—men and women, of different ages (adults 18+ were interviewed), racial groups, economic backgrounds, and geographic locations. Whatever their differences, they shared one thing—they loved Westerns. I updated that research in the summer of 2003 with a survey of another 500 Western fans (for information on the specific methodologies used, see Appendix A). The findings reported in this book are gleaned from both pieces of research. Hundreds of Western fans are quoted, with gender, race, age (in 2004), occupation, and state (or country) where they grew up for each, where the information is available.

So I invite you to share in this discovery, to see for yourself just how diverse this audience is—both in terms of its make-up as well as reasons for loving Westerns. Some stories may ring true for you, some may surprise you. As you read, you may remember parts of your life long forgotten. You may need to put the book down to revisit an old movie friend, or discover a new one. But as you turn each page, know this: If you love Westerns, if the sound of thundering hooves makes your heart race, or the sight of spectacular mountains and canyons catches your breath, or the smell of a campfire takes your cares away, this book is dedicated to you.

CHAPTER 1

WESTERN FANS

John Wayne as Marshal Rooster Cogburn in *True Grit* (1969), courtesy Photofest

When you think of a typical Western fan, what kind of person comes to mind? Do you see a white man in his fifties or older? Is he fairly conservative politically, hard working, with a high school education? As a boy, would he have spent many joyful hours in his local movie theater cheering the good guys and hissing the bad, strapping on his cap guns once he got home to reenact favorite scenes from the day's cinematic action? Today, would he still support everything John Wayne stood for, onscreen and off?

If your answer is yes to any of these questions, you're right…but only to a point.

Did you also think of a black professional who grew up in Harlem in the early 1950s and lived out his Saturday matinee fantasies by sneaking into police stables late at night to ride until all hours? Or a business-woman who grew up singing with Roy Rogers and Dale Evans, refusing to go to school unless she could wear her Annie Oakley guns? How about a Latino rancher descended from a long line of vaqueros who revels in

WESTERN AUDIENCE MATCHES U.S. POPULATION IN KEY AREAS

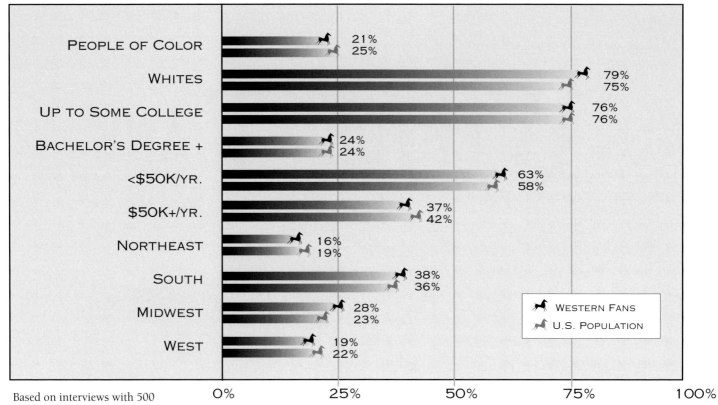

	Western Fans	U.S. Population
PEOPLE OF COLOR	21%	25%
WHITES	79%	75%
UP TO SOME COLLEGE	76%	76%
BACHELOR'S DEGREE +	24%	24%
<$50K/YR.	63%	58%
$50K+/YR.	37%	42%
NORTHEAST	16%	19%
SOUTH	38%	36%
MIDWEST	28%	23%
WEST	19%	22%

Based on interviews with 500 Western fans. U.S. population figures are from 2000 U.S. Census data.

I predict 85% of Western fans will be white, male, conservative, and politically incorrect.

45, white man, Florida

Western fans are bumbling-beer-guzzling-just-a-little-too-lazy-to-ever-leave-the-couch-except-for-commercials-during-Rush-Limbaugh guys.

College student, 20, white man

watching great horsemanship and enjoys Westerns detailing the cattle industry that is her heritage? Or a young man in his early twenties who grew up watching classic Westerns on television with his grandparents and today shares in those dreams of riding the range?

Because all of these, and many more, are Western fans.

There is no such thing as a "typical" Western fan; as a population, Western fans are enormously diverse. Where some might expect them to be almost entirely men, more than one-third (37%) are women. Where some might expect them to be almost entirely white, nearly one-quarter (21%) are people of color. And where some might expect few to have a college education, nearly one-quarter have at least a bachelor's if not a postgraduate degree (24%). In fact, using the U.S. 2000 Census as a base of comparison, Western fans as a group are an *almost exact match* to the U.S. population across a variety of attributes, including race, education, annual household income, and geographic region. The only real differences are gender and age. Men enjoy Westerns at a rate of about two-to-

WESTERN AUDIENCE DIFFERS FROM U.S. POPULATION ON GENDER AND AGE

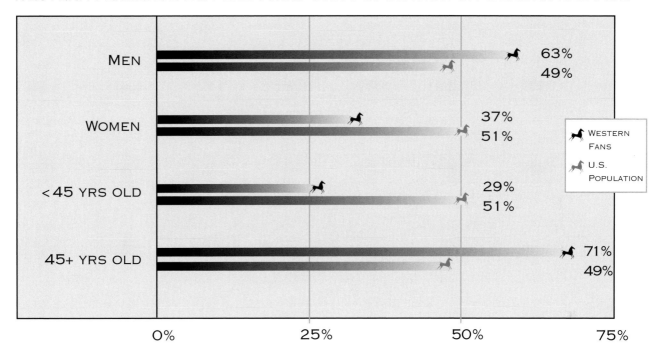

Based on interviews with 500 Western fans. U.S. population figures are from 2000 U.S. Census data.

one over women, and Western fans tend to be older—although, it should be noted, nearly three in ten (29%) are younger than 45 years of age.

That there is such diversity within the Western audience comes as a surprise to many people; the genre has a reputation for promoting a narrow worldview that would, reputably, have little appeal beyond a select audience (e.g., highly conservative, poorly educated white men). To the naysayer, Westerns are violent, representing recklessness and aggression—heroes assert their authority and impose their will at the point of a gun. According to many scholars, the violence in Westerns is justified by the plot—good and evil are delineated in clear, unshakeable terms and the hero has no choice but to act. His use of a gun is powerful, sexy, unmistakably right.

In addition to violence, the Western has been criticized for its representations of women and people of color. And let's be honest—the Western is hardly known for being socially progressive. The heroes of Westerns are almost always white men and it is *their* struggles, crises, decisions, and actions that form the foundation of the genre. White women and people of color function primarily as ancillary characters, necessary presences to define the hero and further the plot, but not complete

American society has stigmatized the Western and influenced many to think of it as an entertainment for the "uncultured," the "uneducated," and the "old-fashioned"! Well, I have two (maybe more) friends (college grads) who verbally affix such stigma to Westerns. However, I have arrived at their house unannounced on more than one occasion to find them engrossed in a Western!

Retired mortgage company president, 69, white man, Mississippi

WESTERN AUDIENCE AS PERCENT OF U.S. POPULATION

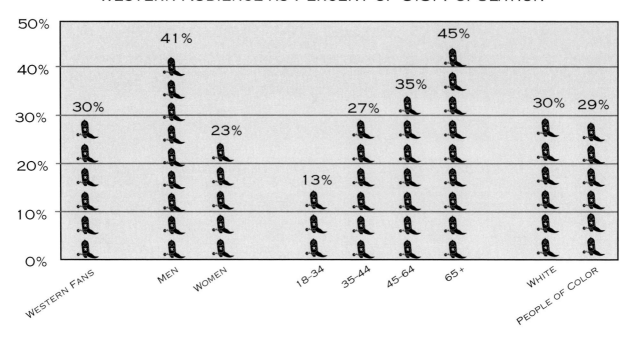

Based on responses from 1677 people

William Holden as Pike Bishop in *The Wild Bunch* (1969), courtesy Photofest

people in and of themselves—women to protect or dominate/win; Indians to kill or serve as helpers; blacks or Asians, if we see them at all, as servants. There are some exceptions, but they are few and far between.

Since the 1970s, when Westerns fell out of favor, the genre has typically been seen and, indeed, widely criticized as operating within the narrow confines just described. In fact, many scholars have characterized it as representing some of the worst tendencies of American culture—an unreconstructed homage to white male machismo, a zealous exaltation of an imagined history that privileges white men, a simplistic celebration of America's frontier past that dramatizes the history of American expansionism as one in which cherished ideals of equality and liberty were never compromised. Critiques in books and academic journals have ranged from the relatively benign—"justification of acts of violent aggression," "exclusionist," "romantic historical reconstructions"—to the highly vituperative—"toxic ethnocentrism," "fantasies of the master race."

And yet, Westerns continue to have a broad appeal. So broad that 30% of American adults today—*that's 57 million people*—from all walks of life, enjoy them. For a genre that has seen only a handful of new movies in the last 30 years and with continually popular classics that arguably represent outdated social mores, that's pretty remarkable! How is this possible?

No one can deny the Western has problematic elements. After all, 4,000 Westerns have been made featuring Indians as villains—painted, war-whooping, tomahawk-wielding, bloodthirsty savages—or quaint, mystical shadows of the past. In fact, few kids growing up playing Cowboys and Indians wanted to be the Indian—that was foisted on younger siblings and friends. As Senator Ben Nighthorse Campbell, a member of the Northern Cheyenne tribe, has stated, "even the Indians didn't want to be Indian."

But…though the Western can certainly be seen as advancing a narrow worldview, it can also be seen as doing something else. At the heart of the Western lie ideals that appeal to and validate the perspectives of a broad base of people—the right to live life on your own terms, the right to stand up and fight for what you believe in, survival against overwhelming odds, loyalty, honor, self-reliance, independence, personal courage, strength, skill. Westerns are also great fun to watch! A delicious combination of elbowroom and heart-thumping action offering uncompromised vistas, pounding hooves, finger-twitching shootouts, those wild open spaces!

It is these elements that account for the widespread popularity of Westerns. People who enjoy them (and moviegoers in general) don't relate

Oh, I was always the Cowboy. We made my sister be the Indian.

　City planner, 51, white
　woman, Rhode Island

Freedom of the open spaces, the horses running free, the guns blazing, that's why I love Westerns. I want to be the good guy sometimes, and the baddie sometimes. Open spaces fascinated me, being a city boy. I dreamed of going West when I was little. I thought it was still like that!

　Helicopter production
　manager, 63, black man,
　Pennsylvania

From left to right, Danny Glover, Kevin Costner, Scott Glenn, Kevin Kline in *Silverado* (1985), courtesy Photofest

Jimmy Stewart as Glyn McLyntock in *Bend of the River* (1952), courtesy Photofest

simply to an actor's gender, race, or age, though those can be important. They relate to attributes, talents, capabilities, skills—John Wayne's refusal to quit in *The Searchers*, William Holden's insistence on loyalty in *The Wild Bunch*. In watching cowboys drive cattle 2,500 miles through storms and stampedes in *Lonesome Dove*, or *The Magnificent Seven* protect Mexican villagers against a band of marauders, fans relate to challenges characters face, journeys and decisions they make, resolutions they come to.

Fans become enchanted by the scenery and music, energized by the action, danger, and good triumphing unconditionally over evil. The hero in a Western may be a white man, but in his stiff-backed resistance to an ever-changing world, in his determination to stand up for his principles and fight to live life on his own terms, in the deep sense of honor compelling him to protect those weaker than himself, to stand fast with his friends, and to do what he knows is right, his struggles are enormously universal—so universal, in fact, many different kinds of people can relate to and identify with him. As this fan comments:

> I love Westerns because I can become a star and participate just by feelings. Using my imagination, I get so involved that I seem to become part of the play. I often wonder how things were during those days. From where I sit, it seemed exciting and challenging. Things were sometimes peaceful and other times wild. Most people were friendly and assisted their fellow man. Others were dominating, manipulating, greedy, thoughtless. I'd loved to have been there, hunting (in sleet or snow), cooking over an open fire, to be next to nature.
>
> Retired public housing authority director, 59, white woman, Louisiana

Those who enjoy Westerns do so for many of the same reasons: the Western's depiction of a historical era they can vicariously experience, its action (horse chases, fistfights, gunplay), its resolute and fearless heroes, its dazzling landscapes, nostalgia for a simpler time (whether an idealized historical past or their own childhoods). Note the similarities in the following remarks on why they love Westerns from people with different backgrounds:

Westerns are real American stories of the West, but also a fantasy trip with heroes you can look up to. Taking you to places and a time you could otherwise never know.

> Preacher/nostalgia dealer, 72, white man, Pennsylvania

Good black and white conflict is always resolved man to man—outdoor action and a closer life to nature—usually beautiful scenery—beautiful old guns.

> Airline mechanic, 64, white man, Illinois

Most Westerns portray real men who would stand up for a cause, family, friends, and their homeland. They are exciting and action packed!

> Postal clerk, 47, black woman, West Virginia

Cowboys, horses, and guns! Westerns have great scenery, lots of action, and the good guys (almost always) win.

> Hospital purchasing manager, 45, white woman, Missouri

Westerns are clean (morally), good entertainment—they remind me of my parents' youth days and help us to reminisce about the way things were—and the way things still should be. Reminds me of the American Dream! I wish Westerns would come back in full force. Western movies, Western shows! Good entertainment, good acting, good clean fun! Living life the cowboy way! They bring out the good in people and help us to remember the way things were—instead of the way things are in this crazy world of today.

> Secretary, 43, white woman, California

In addition to favored attributes, fans also speak consistently of admired *values*: standing up for your principles, right over wrong, freedom, loyalty, honor, courage, determination. Again, note how very different kinds of people can enjoy Westerns for similar reasons:

Usually in Western movies, it's right versus wrong and justice, truth, integrity, honesty prevail. It's the forces of evil, greed, insincerity against the desire to lead a "good life," with real and simple values like love, friendship, etc.

> Ranch trustee, 68, Asian man, Hawaii

I love history and the outdoor life. I would love to be able to travel back in time to see how this country was settled and developed. Being a hunter and outdoorsman, I have always been captivated by the Western way of life and "cowboys." Movie Westerns allow me to live in the Old West vicariously.

> Retired U.S. probation office supervisor, 58, white man, Louisiana

I believe in right and wrong. Big Jake played on what was right! Didn't knuckle under to the bad guys. The good guys went in and kicked some bad guy butt!

> Deputy sheriff, 46, white man, California

Watching my favorite Westerns makes me feel right wins out, justice prevails, the Bad Guys get their just deserts.

> Retired veteran's service officer, 58, black man

I enjoy the way Good and Evil are cast in the play. One knows the strength of Good and that Evil cannot withstand the light that Good sheds. The play is Black and White, no gray, and all know the Hero and the Rat!

> Salesman, 53, Latino man, Colorado

I love Westerns for the simple escapism depicting family values and morals that are found lacking in society today.

   U.S. Army retiree, 65, white man, West Virginia

In writing of their love of Westerns, fans use a nearly universal language: "exciting," "clean," "simple," "honest," "fundamental," "basic," "realistic." They talk about heroes who "stand up for a cause," enjoy what they feel are portrayals of the "American spirit" (self-sufficiency, perseverance, determination), identify with "good morals and values." Despite a common language for enjoying Westerns overall, however, fans gravitate toward movies that speak to them personally, about their own lives, their own experiences, their own perspectives. They are *selective*, engaged by some facets of the genre more than others, as they are engaged by some Westerns more than others. In fact, many will tell you they don't like *all* Westerns. As this fan notes:

> *I prefer Gunslingers to Cowboys (excepting* Lonesome Dove*) and I have trouble with savage Indians, preferring robbers, thieves, and more contemporary "scoundrels."*
>
>   Film student, 20, Asian man, California

Even people we wouldn't expect to enjoy Westerns can have favorites. For example, feminist literary critic and holistic educator Jane Tompkins argues in her book, *West of Everything*, that the Western, as it originally emerged in novel form at the end of the nineteenth century, was *intentionally* designed as a "literary gender war," as she terms it. She makes a provocative case, positioning the genre as inherently anti-woman:

> I think it is no accident that men gravitated in imagination [at the end of the nineteenth century] to a womanless milieu, a set of rituals featuring physical combat and physical endurance, and a social setting that branded most features of civilized existence as feminine and corrupt, banishing them in favor of the three main targets of [late nineteenth century] women's reform: whiskey, gambling, and prostitution.

Given this argument, we might expect Tompkins to be highly critical of the genre. And yet, she is a Western fan. "I make no secret of the fact," she

I have always had a love affair with the West since early childhood. Westerns, cowboys, and American Indians have fascinated me all my life. I enjoy the beauty, the vastness, the endless open range and freedom that the West has. I remember my grandfather taking me to the Saturday matinees and being thrilled by the double features featuring many of my favorite Western heroes in the late '40s and '50s. I love the rugged open-air freedom only the West can provide.

Supermarket manager, 65, white man, Tennessee

Westerns show the power and rugged beauty of the West. The hard yet simple lifestyles and the pure honesty or dishonesty of the people.

Pediatric surgeon, 55, white man, Ohio

I hate injustice and love to see the bad guys get what's coming to them!

Sign maker, 58, white man, California

I don't love all Western movies, but the best among them speak to and of the best in all of us—a refusal to allow bullying, a strong work ethic, the inevitable triumph of good.

Retired English professor, 68, white woman, Michigan

Westerns are exciting, clean; you can watch them with Grandma and not be embarrassed.

Homemaker, 57, white woman, Oklahoma

Westerns make me feel that there were great men in our past who lived by a code that has long disappeared. That code is honor—even the questionable heroes had honor. They lived on the fringe of the law, but they kept the peace. They did not tolerate law-breakers and they made sure that those who broke the law were brought to justice.

Radio marketing and production executive, 53, white man, California

They represent a time when life was more basic. I like values that were held and supported by most people. Life was what you made it, and not what was "given" to you. If things got tough, people went to wherever they needed to go to make their life better (the old "pull yourself up by your bootstraps" idea).

Financial planner, 62, Native American woman, Texas

declares in the opening sentence of her book, "I love Westerns." Almost 40 when she rediscovered the genre via Louis L'Amour novels, she came to realize she identified with the heroes:

> They worked hard, and so did I. They kept going under adverse circumstances, and so did I. Often, after finishing a L'Amour book, I would feel inspired to go back to some difficult task, strengthened in the belief that I could complete it if only I didn't give up. Westerns made me want to work, they made me feel good about working, they gave me what I needed in order to work hard.

As with many Western fans, Tompkins likes to imagine herself as the hero—even if she doesn't admire all of his traits:

> I have felt contempt and hatred for the Western hero, for his self-righteousness, for his silence, for his pathetic determination to be tough, [but] the desire to be the Western hero, with his squint and his silence and his swagger, always returns. I want to be up there in the saddle, looking down at the woman in homespun; I want to walk into the cool darkness of the saloon, order a whiskey at the bar, feel its warmth in my throat, and hear the conversation come to a sudden halt.

We might think Tompkins is unusual—a feminist intellectual with a passion for Westerns. But this is not the case. Native American intellectual and Indian rights advocate Vine Deloria Jr., perhaps best known for his seminal book *Custer Died for Your Sins* (1969), one of the first to examine U.S. race relations, federal bureaucracies, Christian churches, and social scientists from an Indian point of view, also enjoys many Westerns. In a letter to the author, he wrote:

> Most probably, if the filmmaker is aware of it, Western landscape provides a stark, simple, and fundamental physical arena where man meets cosmic forces, at least it provides this context, so that we can explore the meaning of our lives.

Not surprisingly, he has strong objections to certain elements of the genre and is quick to point out he does *not* endorse all Westerns:

> On the whole the casual way that filmmakers treat the Indian subjects is very distasteful to me. There are hundreds of thrilling stories about people in the West and heroic exploits, but film

From left to right in the foreground, Gregory Peck and Skip Homeier in *The Gunfighter* (1950), courtesy Photofest

people seem to rely on a few dramatic story lines that are predictable and consequently Westerns often reinforce conservative fantasies about the world instead of educating people.

Nonetheless, he does have his favorites:

> I like *Junior Bonner* best because it gives such incredibly precise character studies with the major characters. I also like *The Gunfighter* because it illustrates the basic loneliness of human life and the wholly whimsical nature of fate.

Though there are fans who will watch any movie so long as it is a Western, for most, certain movies or certain types of stories resonate more strongly than others. For some, the best Westerns are those depicting a strong and hearty American character, determined pioneers who risked everything to make a better life for themselves and their families—the women who weather enormous hardships to travel from Chicago to Oregon to be wives for settlers in *Westward the Women*, the homesteaders who stand their ground against powerful cattle interests in *Shane*. Others look for Westerns promoting leadership and social responsibility, with characters who from a position of superiority protect those weaker than themselves—John Wayne, Harry Carey Jr., and Pedro Armendariz as three outlaws risking their freedom and their lives trekking across the desert to fulfill a dying woman's request to save her baby in *The Three Godfathers*.

Steve McQueen in the title role, *Junior Bonner* (1972), courtesy Photofest

Fans of such movies as *The Ballad of Little Jo,* with Suzy Amis as a woman who lives her life disguised as a man, may gravitate toward Westerns that emphasize standing up for the right to live life on their own terms, often in defiance of strict social convention, while Clint Eastwood in *The Good, the Bad and the Ugly,* all but crawling across the desert with no water, can offer others tales of survival that pit man against nature. Still others just love to see Western life portrayed—skilled horsemanship in *Rio Grande* as Ben Johnson and Harry Carey Jr., in a stunt they performed themselves, race across the desert each standing astride two galloping horses; the awe-inspiring mountainous panorama revealed as Scott Glenn opens the door from his dark, cramped cabin early in *Silverado.*

These various attributes and themes can resonate strongly for fans in different Westerns or, more interesting, even in the same movie. In fact, Western fans often enjoy the *same* movie, but for completely *different* reasons. This can play out in unexpected ways. For example, a 50-year-old white man from Arizona with a bachelor's degree, a letter carrier for

Westerns are American mythology involving character, obligation, courage, willingness to go alone against the odds, uplifting.

Retired electrical engineer, 79, white man, Australia

The macho fantasy is always appealing. Westerns always conjure up a way of life I will never know—making your own rules. The raw power of being willing to die for your beliefs, your horse, your land, your self-respect. It was a man's world. I can relax in movie theaters.

Nanny, 59, white woman, Michigan

From left to right, John Wayne, Harry Carey Jr., and Pedro Armendariz in *The Three Godfathers* (1948), courtesy Photofest

the U.S. Postal Service, loves Westerns because he admires American pioneers' perseverance and determination, traits he feels Westerns dramatize authentically:

> *The positive traits of Western characters are the same that have caused our nation to prosper and made America synonymous with greatness. The West was settled by people who, for a variety of reasons, challenged a new land. Good or bad, they HAD to have courage just to have dared. Shirkers and cowards some may have been, but they did it nonetheless.*

Shane (1953) is his favorite Western because it illustrates for him what the pioneer spirit is all about—strength, resolve, persistence. He especially enjoys:

> *…the scene in which Shane and the farmer Starrett use every physical force available to them to pull up the stump of a tree to clear land for a crop, as it is another indication of perseverance and determination that is an American character.*

For this man, *Shane* encapsulates a vision of the pioneer that accounts for America's greatness:

> *…each character skillfully portraying people we know were real. It took all they had, but they did it. Free enterprise. Clear the land and you can grow crops to feed your family and prosper.*

As a man with conservative politics, against gun control and government bureaucracy, he sees "real people" who took advantage of opportunity and, through sheer perseverance and determination, succeeded. "Has anything changed?" he laments, "well, they didn't have continued governmental interference to contend with." Personal courage and fortitude engage this man, the idea of pushing yourself and prevailing, free from arbitrary and inane restriction. He loves Westerns because, for him, Westerns show pioneers who tamed a wilderness and created a great, thriving nation.

Quite different from this man is another Western fan who picks *Shane* as his favorite, a 58-year-old white man with a Ph.D. in English literature. He is a university professor originally from Indiana who loved Westerns as a boy because he could get lost in the action and adventure, while

From left to right, Alan Ladd, Van Heflin, Jean Arthur in *Shane* (1953), courtesy Photofest

today their beautiful landscapes not only strongly appeal to, but rejuvenate him:

> I grew up in the '50s. As a boy in the '50s, it was very difficult to find a "mythos" which was as friendly, as comforting, and as adventurous as the Western. The movie Western was one way in which I could imaginatively enter a familiar world and participate in the action. Since then, I have become familiar with the geographic West and I love the country. Movie Westerns give me a chance to return to landscape which I find restoring!

Shane is his favorite Western because it speaks to him personally on several different levels:

> Shane conjures up all sorts of emotions and values which somehow relate to me in a personal way: the concept of the loner, the concept of not letting anyone bully another person, the concept of surviving against overwhelming odds, and the concept of disappearing into

Alan Ladd in the title role, *Shane* (1953), courtesy Photofest

nature. Shane, the character, ultimately turns his back on civilization and returns to the mountains, even though he has made the situation possible for civilization to prosper. I always hoped (and still do) that the boy does not wait for Shane to come back, but that he takes off after him and never returns to his parents!

"As a gay man," he writes, "I am especially concerned with issues dealing with the gay male and female minority," and finds within the genre attributes articulating his point of view—images of survival and strength, validation of the outsider's status, the right of self-assertion, and the fantasy of riding off and leaving civilization behind.

A 50-year-old Native American man of Rosebud Sioux heritage also chooses *Shane* as his favorite Western. He is a teacher's aide with a high school diploma and credits toward a bachelor's degree. He has a more complex relationship with Westerns, as we might expect, given that he is a Native American, but even more so for having grown up in a mission boarding school where children were forced to cut their hair and severely punished for speaking their native languages and practicing their native religions. As to why he loves Westerns, he relates an experience common to many Native Americans:

I love Westerns because it was drilled into me at the mission boarding school (and I actually cheered for the U.S. Cavalry when they appeared in the nick of time).

Given this comment, we might assume he wouldn't enjoy Westerns as an adult. But this isn't the case—he loves *Shane*. Why? As he writes:

None of my Indian people were involved and it showed how a man attempted to change, but had to resort to his old ways to save his fellow men who were being exploited by others of the same race. Also the feeling that one man can often make a difference, even if it means going back to his former profession.

The political issue of most importance to this man is religious freedom—"we don't object to the Catholic Church when they have mass, baptism, etc., so I would like them to respect our way of worshipping God"—and he sees within *Shane* elements that validate his point of view: "resorting to old ways to save his fellow men," making a difference by "going back to his former profession." There are certainly things about Westerns this man does not like—in fact, one reason he chooses *Shane* as his favorite is there are no Indians in it—but the movie nonetheless offers him something that is personally meaningful.

These are three *very* different men. They have different backgrounds, different experiences, different views—the letter carrier served six years' active duty in the navy and holds the rank of lieutenant commander in the active reserves, the university professor has no military experience, and the teacher's aide opposed the Vietnam War. In fact, that they choose *Shane* as their favorite movie Western may be one of the only things these men have in common. And yet, each finds personal significance in this movie—pride in the American character, validation of the outsider, value of "old ways."

From left to right in the foreground, Alan Ladd and Ben Johnson in *Shane* (1953), courtesy Photofest

Clearly, fans relate to favorite Westerns in many different ways. What's so surprising, though, is not so much that one Western can mean different things to different people (after all, when was the last time you and a friend agreed about every aspect of a movie?), but just how *very* different, and how very *personalized*, those meanings can be across a *highly diverse* group of people. Loving Westerns is not simply a matter of a niche audience watching old shoot-em-ups. Loving Westerns is a dynamic, vibrant cultural phenomenon that continues into the present day. Loving Westerns is something, despite our differences, many Americans (not to mention people in other countries) share.

A SHARED LEGACY

Western fans love the Old West and what many relate to as the "frontier spirit." It is a common language, a common understanding, a common ideal (however romanticized). To Western fans, the "frontier" means freedom, strength, indomitability, courage, perseverance—not to mention a good dose of adventure mixed in!

> *I love watching the stamina and guts the people had for adventure, travel, and hardship in order to survive.*
>   Business manager, 56, white woman, Montana

Many Western fans are drawn to the idea of the frontier—the spirit of it, the character of it, the rawness of it—galloping free across the plains, persevering despite great adversity and personal tragedy, triumphing against seemingly insurmountable odds. In our mind's eye, we see the Texacan settlers in *The Searchers* battling forces, both human and natural, to create a legacy for future generations, or Robert Redford in *Jeremiah Johnson* as the famed mountain man who, tired of the trappings of civilization, sets out to conquer the wilderness.

To identify with the frontier legacy, whether through Western novels, movies, or television shows, is to claim the frontier heritage as your own, to place yourself within a highly valued cultural tradition that is fundamentally American—taking a risk to make a better life for your

family, overcoming hardship, standing up for what you believe in (even if that belief goes against the fashion), fighting for the right to live life on your own terms. The frontier is a history and a legacy that we—all of us—share.

A Shared Experience

Most fans grew up watching Westerns, whether in darkened theaters rooting for their favorite B cowboys to win the day, or in their living rooms tuning in every week to favorite television series. When they weren't watching Westerns, many conquered a wilderness, building forts, crossing prairies, and surviving flood, famine, and disease—all within the confines of their own backyards and streets.

Always enjoyed Westerns, ever since I was a little fella. We played Cowboys and Indians. We used to pull a big old limb off the tree. We'd

I grew up on Westerns in the '30s. I was the oldest of four children. I took my two brothers and one sister to the show every Saturday afternoon. (It gave my mother the only peace she had all week.) I can still hear the screams and cheers as the cowboy hero (who didn't drink or swear) fought, captured, or arrested the crooks!

Retired minister, 82, white man, Oklahoma

I remember, with pleasure, being a little girl and curling up beside Dad in his chair and watching the Westerns on the black and white. I felt safe and comfortable.

Director of Title III programs, 47, white woman, Illinois

I remember watching TV Westerns with my dad. He loved the adventure represented on the screen. After watching so many and reading so many Louis L'Amour, he predicted action very accurately and we had an unspoken contest to predict how the story would end.

Retired elementary school teacher, 63, white man, Rhode Island

I was born Western—I was riding horses around Buffalo, WY, by the time I was two.

Retired teacher, 82, white woman, Wyoming

We grew up around cowboys and Indians. Westerns bring back a lot of memories to me because I lived in the West— saw wild horse roundups, went to Indian rodeos, and cowboy rodeos. Also my brother and I would go to the Indian village at night and watch them play their games and listen to the drums.

Homemaker, 74, white woman, Washington

throw a rope around the branch where it was bare and the leaves would be behind us like the horse's tail, and we'd run all over that dirt road. There'd be a bunch of us, five or six of us.

Truck driver for a recycling company, 55, black man, Alabama

Generations of people (beginning in the late nineteenth century) grew up with Westerns. Through Westerns, they bonded with their culture, bonded with their friends, and bonded with their families—in fact, fathers played an especially important role in this last piece. Many fans talk emotionally about the special times they spent with fathers or grandfathers enjoying the West of the silver screen. In a culture where men are (or at least were) not free to show their children or grandchildren open affection, many developed a strong bond through the shared experience of watching Westerns.

Westerns remind me about past times. I watched Westerns growing up with Grandpop there. That's all Grandpop ever watched, so I grew to like J. Wayne, too.

Farmer, 21, black man, Missouri

Some Western fans came up with more than the West of popular culture; raised in a rural environment and/or as descendents of westerners (e.g., Indians, cowboys, ranchers, pioneers, miners, lawmen), they bring to their love of Westerns the double experience of having grown up with the movies as well as their own family history. Again, note the variety of types of people sharing this experience:

My family were pioneers, strong of heart. They wouldn't tolerate our society today. They would clean out the herd. Quickly.

Stunt actor/rancher, 72, white man, Texas

It reminds me of my background. My father was, and two brothers are, real cowboys. There is some excitement in riding horses and working cattle. All this excitement and pride is relived when I see a good Western movie.

Retired teacher, 61, Latino woman, Texas

Watching my favorite Westerns evokes a wildness in me and a peace-

From left to right, Dale Evans, Trigger, and Roy Rogers, publicity still c. late 1940s, used by permission of The Roy Rogers-Dale Evans Museum

I grew up on a ranch and cowboys were a part of my life. My grandfather was a true frontiersman and cowboy. He raised horses and mules for the Army up to the Korean War. My father felt you should be allowed to do whatever you were big enough to handle. I have been "thrown" many times, but I always get back on. A real feeling of belonging and doing is what Westerns are about.

Small manufacturing company owner, 59, white man, Texas

ful feeling. At times an emotion of fretfulness overcomes me—a mixture of excitement, of challenge and calmness—maybe because of the long line of Choctaw Indians in my family line.

Retired public housing authority director, 59, Native American woman, Louisiana

In today's popular culture, dominated by action-packed summer blockbusters, youth-oriented comedies, and horror/slasher films, it's easy to forget that generations of Americans, enamored with the West of the silver screen, dreamed of becoming cowboys. That thread, though not as visible today, is still very strong. For many fans, Westerns are heavily nostalgic.

I have always loved Nature and the great outdoors—mountains, etc., and especially the West. In fact, when I was growing up, I wanted to be a cowboy.

Homemaker, 92, white woman, North Carolina

Kurt Russell as Wyatt Earp, *Tombstone* (1993), courtesy Photofest

A SHARED VISION OF BEHAVIOR

Many fans today admire and want to emulate their favorite movie Western heroes—John Wayne saving Jimmy Stewart and elevating him to heroic status by killing Lee Marvin's evil gunman from the shadows in *The Man Who Shot Liberty Valance*, Kurt Russell avenging the death of his younger brother in *Tombstone*. Whether it's personal courage in facing a fight, protecting others, making decisions in the blink of an eye, or just the downright "cool" factor, Western heroes impress and thrill their fans with everything from that steely-eyed stare signaling quick and deadly action to that wry humor bringing a knowing smile.

I like to see good triumph over evil. I like to see the strong help defend the rights of the weak. I like the chivalry. I like the disregard for personal safety sacrificed to save another person or an ideal. I feel that fearless bravery is a dying thing in our world.

Chemical plant worker, 60, white man, Illinois

The code of the hero—honor, loyalty, being true to your word, protecting the weak, not looking for trouble but being prepared to handle it—is a vision of behavior many people relate to. They fantasize about what it would be like to command such respect, be so skilled, so powerful. For many fans, watching favorite scenes is a vicarious experience. It can even be a personal test: What would I do? Would I face the challenge or run? Conquer my fears and save the day or freeze and skulk away?

It allows all of us to live out a fantasy of always standing firm on our convictions, and to be better for it. The good survives. When you put yourself mentally into the shoes (or boots) of the main character, you are extending your own persona into the character and see your own reactions, and ask, "Could I have been that firm?" "Would I have done that?"

Retired chemical plant worker, 60, white man, Illinois

The history of people moving West and the hardships they faced makes me wonder if I could have done it.

Retired bookkeeper, 71, white woman, Illinois

When bullets are flying, who knows what we will do or be capable of. Heroism or walk away begin with the first step.

Baker, 50, white man, Oregon

Westerns bring out feelings of freedom, adventure, sense of dedication to a cause, be it family, morals, punching cows or another person. It is great to think just how you would have been in some of the same situations. Be it one of the good guys or a glorified bad guy.

Office manager, 54, white woman, Texas

Watching a Western leaves me in awe of how many hardships people endured and yet survived. It makes me realize how strong my ancestors must have been, and I wonder if I could have done as well.

U.S. probation office supervisor, 58, white man, Louisiana

Makes me wonder if I have the courage to stand up for what is right.

Stockbroker, 63, white man, Massachusetts

John Wayne as Sheriff John T. Chance in *Rio Bravo* (1959), courtesy Photofest

When all is said and done, Western fans are not a "breed unto themselves." They are a highly diverse audience. Some no doubt look at Westerns and see a comfortable "natural order of things" that validates a conservative worldview with white men enjoying a position of superiority. Others, however, look at the very same movies and see, not a world elevating one group of people at the expense of others, but a world promoting individual strength, perseverance, and courage in a natural setting that allows people who don't necessarily fit into prescribed social roles to be true to themselves.

In a world where we focus so much on our differences, loving Westerns is something many of us share.

Clockwise from top, James Coburn, Brad Dexter, Charles Bronson, Robert Vaughn, Horst Buchholz, Yul Brynner, and Steve McQueen enjoying a light moment on the set of *The Magnificent Seven* (1960), courtesy Photofest

CHAPTER 2

FRONTIER SPIRIT

A family migrating West takes their raft down the wrong fork of a river. The raft is pulverized by rapids and the parents die, but the children go on…

A cattleman with a small group of men drives 10,000 head over unproven trails. Several men are lost to the dust, heat, and a stampede, but the remaining outfit makes trail's end…

From left to right, Carroll Baker and Debbie Reynolds in *How the West Was Won* (1962), courtesy Photofest

Four aging outlaws, trailed by a former associate, try in vain to secure enough money to retire. Facing their own mortality, and unable to stand by while a younger member of their gang is brutally treated by a rogue general, they choose the manner of their own deaths, going out in a blaze of glory…

The Western is basic. An individual, or group of individuals, faced with great hardship, grapples with fundamental issues of survival, loyalty, and honor in the midst of magnificent yet ominous landscape. One wrong move, one wrong decision marks the difference between heroism and cowardice, life and death.

The Western is visceral. We hear the creak of leather and the thunder of hooves. We taste the sweat, the cold beans, and the stale coffee. We feel the wind beating on our faces, the dust stinging our eyes, and the cold rain chilling us to the bone. We smell the horses, the campfires, and the flesh burning under a branding iron.

The Western is straightforward. Stories are not complicated—an individual is challenged and survives or fails. There is no gray area, no social complexity. Hardship, struggle, personal courage, and perseverance—that's what we look for in a Western.

Westerns represent hard times, simple times, people who made the country with backbone and raw nerves.

Customer service supervisor, 52, black woman, Alabama

Westerns contain within them tales of daring and risk—characters undertake perilous journeys to better their lives. They make difficult decisions, but stand up for their principles. They sacrifice, but, in the end, endure and succeed. The West in this context is a universal testing ground, reducing life to its basic elements: survival, loyalty, dignity, righteousness, honor. The Western articulates what many believe makes America unique: that the nation was founded and built by individuals who met the "frontier challenge" and prevailed.

The Western era was a time of new beginnings. Men and women were more independent back then, more self-sufficient, and they were proud to be Americans. Westerners had backbone! The very best Western movies are those that reflect these qualities.

Novelist, 33, white man, Texas

Without a doubt, Westerns romanticize the frontier experience—and so do Western fans. Over and over, fans envision a time when, "unlike today," people successfully stood up for and defended what was right. A time when, "unlike today," people were free to go where they pleased. A time when, "unlike today," people banded together and helped one another.

Westerns—good ones—are emotional experiences. They touch and spark primal feelings because the environments and settings that the characters find themselves in are usually hostile, unyielding—either because of the terrain and untamed wilderness, or because of hostile human forces, or both. Protagonists struggle for survival, identity, and/or integrity against the most basic of challenges, stripped of politics, economics, and social niceties.

Retail banker, 54, black woman, Kansas

I love Westerns for the ruggedness, the quick decisions that mean life or death, the swift justice, and the freedom from so many restrictions that we have today. The way good almost always wins out over evil.

Retired state liquor store manager, 71, white man, North Carolina

Life was very hard, dirty, and long days in the saddle!

Retired secretary, 64, white woman, Maryland

I like seeing portrayals of people working to build towns, railroads, ranches, etc. I love seeing law-abiding people stand up to lawless people.

Federal law enforcement officer, 58, white man, Arkansas

Replenishing water supplies in *Westward the Women* (1951), starring Robert Taylor, Denise Darcel, Hope Emerson, and Henry Nakamura, courtesy Photofest

Westerns portray a more moral and simple time when decisions were made, choices taken, based on fact and emotion, not bureaucracy. Circumstances were more in focus—not blurred by law and societal constraints.

Administrative staff/supervisor, 59, white woman, Virginia

They reflect an era in America that was simpler and where good always triumphed over evil.

Retired engineer, 66, Latino man, New York

I like the way they took on life and faced it. Did what they had to do to get the job done, didn't worry about who the heck they embarrassed in the process, didn't have to fight damn government regs to create jobs, towns, and a great country. You made your own way and weren't looking for a handout! The immigrants fit in or left. This is America, no other country. Be American or go back elsewhere. Fit in with what we're building or split!

President/partner in wholesale building materials business, 59, white man, Minnesota

I am in awe of their perseverance through floods, drought, Indians. Almost everyone lost one or two children due to disease or accident. They left their families and possessions behind to travel unknown territory with no guarantee of success. Everyone chipped in to help each other raise a barn, sew a quilt, harvest fields, brand cattle. If a person gave you their word on something, you knew he would uphold it. If someone did wrong, it was an eye for an eye.

Coal miner, 49, white woman, Wyoming

Westerns give me pride in humanity—when right prevails over wrong—the bad guys get their just rewards. That someone will stand up to the oppressors.

Retired security supervisor, 66, white man, Mississippi

.

I love Westerns because they all take place in a time when man was really free!

31, white man, New York

I love Westerns for the freedom people (male and female) had in that time, or so it appeared.

Lab technician, 47, Native American man, Rhode Island

Westerns give me a sense of total independence and freedom. There were not a whole lot of rules and laws in the Old West.

Retired from the Navy, 52, white man, Indiana

You have a feeling of freedom and space and an ability to roam about as you pleased. A time when love and commitment were strong and clear and the same thing. Honor, duty to others and country.

Disabled, 58, white woman, Colorado

I have always been fascinated by the Old West. Watching Westerns gives me a sense of what life at that time was like. The people, men and women, were strong-minded. They worked hard to keep alive.

Paralegal, 59, white woman, New York

Westerns show a simpler time when Family Values meant something, people worked together, helped one another, people were friendlier. I love horses and the fact that you could build your own home wherever you wanted. People looked out for one another.

Hotel front desk agent, 57, Latino woman, New York

Fans love Westerns because Westerns give them a sense of "being there." For many, Westerns conform to what they believe the Old West was "really" like, giving them "honest" portrayals of people and events.

I love Westerns for the believably Western life! Hard lives of the pioneers brought to audiences.

Salesperson, 33, Latino woman, California

I find them entertaining from a historical viewpoint. Watching them gives me the sense that I've been there and can understand how hard life was back then.

Truck driver, 62, white man, Nebraska

But what is this "honesty," this "reality"? Certainly against any comprehensive historical standard, Westerns fall far short of presenting America's late frontier history in all its complexity—the fact that 30% to 50% of cowboys were men of color, for example, has been almost completely eliminated from the West of the silver screen. So has the broad reality that the "frontier" was not simply a line that moved from east to west following Anglo-European settlement, but a large geographic area where many cultures met—Indians already in place, Spanish and Mexicans coming from the south, Asians from the west, and European immigrants, Anglo-Americans, and blacks coming from the east.

Even the most diehard Western fans will admit Westerns can play footloose and fancy free with historic precision.

Even though I realize that most Westerns exaggerate what it was like in the old West, it gives us some idea of what it was like.

29, white woman, Massachusetts

Many, however, don't realize by just how much. Statistics show that Abilene, Caldwell, Ellsworth, Dodge City, and Wichita, for example,

Vaqueros, c. 1885, author's collection

averaged as few as 1.5 deaths each per season throughout their heyday as railroad heads during the cattle driving era (1870-1885)—not what we would expect given the hundreds of shootouts we've "seen" on those dusty streets. In fact, a cowboy was more at risk of having a fatal accident on horseback, getting tangled in his own rope or stirrup, than dying in a gunfight. Similarly, the death rate among overland migrants may have been much less than we have come to expect; as few as 3% of pioneers died as they made the trek in covered wagons across the continent, and 90% of *those* died of disease, particularly cholera. Then, of course, there has been the cinematic representation of Indian/white relations. Whites have been portrayed as righteous avengers, rarely the aggressors, whereas Indians have been the savages who stood in the way of civilization. There have been exceptions to this, but not many.

And yet, for the majority of Western fans, the very concept of "The West" connotes a vision of vast, untrammeled expanses, excitement, and

The amusing part for me is to watch how the attitudes of any given era ('30s, '40s, '50s, etc.) are reflected in the filmmaking, dialog, wardrobe, etc., thus producing a distorted view of "the West," leading people to believe—"That's how it really was!"

Fitness instructor/horse riding guide/film production assistant, 51, white woman, California

Westerns are a general glimpse of our American past. A small snapshot of who we were and a little of how we got to be who we are as a people and a nation. Not always a complete or accurate picture, but, after all, it is entertainment, not a documentary.

Computer Aided Design (CAD) developer, 51, white woman, Kansas

I have that romantic idea that ranch life would be fun and rewarding (I actually know better), so enjoy seeing it portrayed on-screen.

Bookkeeper, 62, white woman, Colorado

I have always enjoyed the action, adventure, and qualities portrayed in Westerns. Even though I know the difference now between what is legend and what is fact, as well as fictional characters, I still enjoy Westerns. As a child I wanted to be a cowboy.

Judge, 56, white man, New York

They depict a young United States population struggling to develop the Wild West where only the survival of the fittest was the general rule. There was also total freedom to do whatever you wanted to do out in the West. You could always build a better life for yourself and there were always plenty of opportunities to take advantage of. Being in the West was always a total adventure.

Retired from the Navy, 52, white man, Indiana

They remind me of a time when things were simple and new, but that life could be tough and adventurous (not as much as Hollywood would have us believe). The idea that a man could move West, stake out a piece of land, and "start afresh" is a concept that formed the American pioneer spirit. I think that a bit of that spirit resides in some of us even today. That's what makes Westerns appealing to us.

College bookstore employee, 36, white woman, Mississippi

They reflect the history of this country. Geronimo attempts to actually reflect the historical events in an accurate fashion. It brings up concern for the Indians today and their future survival.

Human resources executive, 62, black woman, New York

unlimited opportunity hampered only by individual shortcomings. The often brutal realities of hardship, inequality, failure, and loss are superseded by a mythology that promises unlimited opportunity, the right to live life on your own terms, and absolute freedom. Favorite Westerns are, for many fans, "accurate," "real," "believable," "authentic," "educational." They show "people we know were real," depicting "a way of life" as it "actually was." In fact, "authenticity" or "realism" is the number one reason people love Westerns—more than action, more than heroes, more than nostalgia, horses, and landscape combined.

> *They keep alive the spirit that expanded our nation. Westerns reflect the rugged individualism and courage of those who sacrificed so much to fill dreams of owning their own land, gold, finding a mate, or whatever drove them from civilization into unknown adventure.*

Newspaper writer/photographer, 65, white woman, California

What that "accuracy" is, however, has more to do with individual perspective than it does history. Yes, many Western fans insist on at least a modicum of historic accuracy—don't drive cattle up the Chisholm Trail in 1899, don't shoot Winchester 92s in a picture set in 1880 (many

Crossing the arid landscape in *Stagecoach* (1939), courtesy Photofest

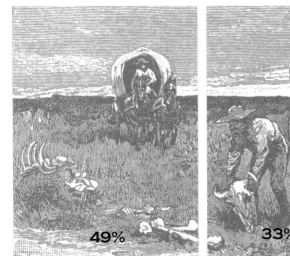

49%	33%	30%	13%	11%	11%	11%
Authenticity/Realism	Action	Heroes/ good over evil	Nostalgia for a simpler time	Horses	Land- scape	Grew up on them

hardware aficionados enjoy watching—and critiquing—firearm accuracy), don't tell one-sided stories (e.g., include Native American perspectives, the contributions of blacks, Asians, Latinos). Though most Westerns are true to broad historical events and trends (and some Westerns do this better than others), history serves as just the basis from which storytellers select and embellish their tales. Log cabins, wagon trains, dusty towns, Indian villages, great herds of cattle, mountain rendezvous, rushing rivers, plains of undulating grass, red rock monoliths and canyons—these are the Western's settings, props, and environments. They must be there for a movie to succeed as a Western.

But to be a *believable* Western, it must have more. Even if the setting is right, a Western must also represent the *spirit* of the frontier as we understand it. If it fails to do that, then it truly fails as a Western, no matter how "accurate" the setting. Think of *Red River*, with John Wayne as a single-minded rancher who, starting with nothing, builds a great herd and is the first to drive cattle north from Texas to Kansas. Or *Wagon Master*, staring Ward Bond as a guide who leads a group of social outcasts, mostly Mormons, as they struggle to cross forbidding landscape to reach their promised land. Such movies embody this spirit, one rooted in cherished ideals and character traits more than cold hard facts: the rewards that

Based on interviews with 500 Western fans; Interviewees could list more than one reason, so percents add up to more than 100.

My interest in Westerns waned in the 60s/70s—I started picking up the hardware errors. Then there was Clint in Unforgiven. *Wow, it was like getting hit with a brick to wake you up! My favorite part was the authentic and varied guns. A Smith and Wesson Schofield? Whoever used an S&W in a Western movie before?*

Mechanical engineer, 64, white man, Rhode Island

come with hard work, the possibility of great achievement from humble beginnings, determination, fortitude, ingenuity.

Of course, in many respects, this notion of a frontier spirit is rooted in fact—what else but persistence and determination could drive people to leave their families and communities and enable them to survive such a harsh environment, successfully building a new home literally from the "ground up"? But, overall, history has yielded to an ideal, and this ideal has *become* our reality, our historic truth. The frontier spirit is something many perceive as uniquely and definingly American, at once indomitable and rugged, but also lively and fun-loving—Debbie Reynolds and Carroll Baker as two sisters who live their lives against the expanse of frontier history in *How the West Was Won*. The West of this vision can be harsh and unyielding, but also free-spirited, thrilling, and carefree. It is an image that enthralls, inspires, and uplifts.

There is certainly nothing new in pointing out that Westerns romanticize America's frontier past. But this is deeply embedded in our culture. In fact, a highly romanticized frontier experience has been part of the American landscape for *more than 100 years*—and hasn't come just from fiction writers and filmmakers. Artists, as early as the 1830s, were producing paintings and lithographs ennobling America's frontier character. From early representations of pioneers traveling West through late nineteenth-century depictions of cowboy and frontier life (from such celebrated painters/sculptors as Frederick Remington and Charles Russell), artists played a large role as early proponents of an idealized history.

The frontier spirit received early intellectual and political validity as well. Historian Frederick Jackson Turner delivered his famous paper on the frontier's significance to an audience of his colleagues at the Columbia Exposition in Chicago in 1893. Titled "The Significance of the Frontier in American History," Turner contended the frontier experience defined American development and the American character. "The existence of an area of free land, its continuous recession, and the advance of American settlement westward," he wrote, "explain American development." His use of the terms "westward" and "free land" here are notable. They assume, first, the American frontier was "settled" on an east to west trajectory; second, the land was unoccupied; and, finally, homesteaders didn't

have to pay for land once the native peoples were removed. The truth is, railroads were the nation's largest landowners by 1871 and only about one acre in nine went directly to pioneers. Most had to pay $2 to $15 per acre to investors or speculators, a hefty price for generally poor farmers in the late 1800s who were looking to work a good-sized homestead.

Turner went on to point out the frontier experience also bred particular character traits:

> …that coarseness and strength combined with acuteness and acquisitiveness; that practical inventive turn of mind, quick to find expedients; that masterful grasp of material things, that restless, nervous energy; that dominant individualism.

This is a familiar evocation, but not one we would necessarily expect from a *historian*—a vision of free land, a frontier line receding to the advance of American settlement, combined with individual strength, courage, and perseverance. It is an evocation of determination, survival, and triumph—and one that has played out in countless Westerns over the years.

President Theodore Roosevelt inspecting Yellowstone National Park, 1903, courtesy Harvard College Library

Outside academic circles, Turner's thesis received little attention at the time, but other more visible late nineteenth/early twentieth-century American leaders played a key role in propagating an idealized Western past. Theodore Roosevelt was himself enamored of the Western ideal, having spent two years, from 1884 to 1886, on his own ranch in the Dakota territory. In his 1888 memoir of those years, *Ranch Life and the Hunting Trail*, he described cowboys as:

...hardy and self-reliant as any men who ever breathed—with bronzed, set faces, and keen eyes that look all the world in the faces, and without flinching. Except while on sprees, they are quiet, rather self-contained men, perfectly frank and simple. There is a high regard for truthfulness and keeping one's word, intense contempt for any kind of hypocrisy, and a hearty dislike of a man who shirks his work. The cowboy will not submit tamely to an insult, nor has he an overwrought fear of shedding blood. He does possess, to a very high degree, the stern, manly qualities that are invaluable to a nation.

With historians and national leaders extolling an idealized West (and western*er*), no wonder the line between historical accuracy and a romanticized past became so blurred!

Of course, artists, writers, intellectuals, and political leaders weren't the only ones popularizing an idealized frontier experience at the end of the nineteenth century. The Western's format—exhilarating exploits, death-defying feats, ferocious hand-to-hand combat, eleventh-hour rescues—was also well-established by then. Dime novelists set the foundation in the 1860s, but the genre's construction had its most successful propagator in Buffalo Bill Cody and his Wild West Show. William Frederick Cody was born in Iowa in 1846 and, by age 20, had worked as a wrangler, Pony Express rider, stagecoach driver, army scout, and buffalo hunter (known widely for his expert marksmanship, hence his nickname). In 1872, Cody made his first appearance on stage in a drama created by famed dime novelist Ned Buntline. *The Scouts of the Prairie* featured Cody as well as Buntline and another well-known scout, Texas Jack Omohundro. Cody and Omohundro (playing themselves) brought a realism to the stage that helped make the play a success.

Buffalo Bill, c. 1887, courtesy Buffalo Bill Historical Center, Cody, Wyoming; P.69.2088

BUFFALO BILL'S WILD WEST·
CONGRESS, ROUGH RIDERS OF THE WORLD.

MISS ANNIE OAKLEY,
THE PEERLESS LADY WING-SHOT.

Wild West Show poster, courtesy Buffalo Bill Historical Center, Cody, Wyoming; gift of the Coe Foundation; 1.69.73

The Western movie depicts the nineteenth century, whether accurately or not. One of my feelings is that I would like to have been around to see it. The idea of space, that one could pick up and leave for some undisturbed spot in the country has an attraction. I'm sure life was just as boring and tedious in the nineteenth century, but not so in a Western movie!

Library worker, 65, white man, Rhode Island

I would have liked (or maybe I did) to have lived during that time frame. "Wild and free on the great prairie!"

Teacher/coach, 61, white man, Rhode Island

Bitten by the show business bug, Cody organized his own troupe the following season, which, ten years later (in 1883), became Buffalo Bill's Wild West Show. It was an outdoor spectacle with a cast of *hundreds*, including Indian chiefs and warriors (Sitting Bull appeared for one season), sharpshooters (notably Annie Oakley), and cowboys (some of whom went on to work in the budding film industry), as well as live buffalo, elk, and cattle. For 30 years, spectators gasped at and cheered dramatizations of "real" Western events—buffalo hunts, Pony Express rides, wagon train journeys, an Indian attack on the Deadwood stagecoach, a reenactment of Custer's Defeat (featuring some Lakota who had participated in the battle). Hundreds of thousands, if not millions of people nationally and internationally saw the show, including Queen Victoria on the occasion of her Golden Jubilee. By 1900, Buffalo Bill Cody was reputedly the most famous American in the world.

This nineteenth century vision of the frontier—free land, adventure, hardy pioneers, roaming cowboys, righteous and honorable people forging a nation—is remarkably unchanged today. On January 21, 1985, President Ronald Reagan concluded his second inaugural address with the following remarks:

> History is a ribbon, always unfurling; history is a journey. And as we continue our journey, we think of those who traveled before us. Now we hear again the echoes of our past: the men of the Alamo call out encouragement to each other; a settler pushes west and sings a song, and the song echoes out forever and fills the unknowing air. It is the American sound. It is hopeful, big-hearted, idealistic, daring, decent, and fair. That's our heritage; that is our song. We sing it still. For all our problems, our differences, we are together as of old.

Many Western fans see the history of the frontier within this vision, as the quintessential expression of the American experience, the American character. For them, the frontier encapsulates in the broadest sense what it *means* to be an American: integrity, resourcefulness, unlimited opportunity. They yearn for a time they perceive to be simpler, where choices were more fundamental, people lived closer to nature, were free to move about as they pleased, and were judged by their capabilities, not by titles or other markers of social standing (e.g., property ownership, money, family background, gender, race).

In fact, the "Old West" of the popular imagination is so idealized that, for many fans, the line between mythology and historic reality is barely distinguishable, if it exists at all. Note the remarks from the following Western fan:

> *When I see my favorite Western,* Dances with Wolves, *I always imagine what life would have been like for me during that period. Not as a black woman, but a time where the color of a person's skin was unimportant.*

> Administrative assistant, 54, black woman, Illinois

Even after admitting "I am a romantic, I guess!" this black woman believes that in the historic West, the color of a person's skin was *unimportant.* A time of oppressive racial barriers that were codified into law via strict rules of segregation (there were separate saloons and dance halls in Western towns for whites and "coloreds"), when violence against people of color reached a nearly unprecedented level (through individual acts of brutality, starvation, military and militia attacks, lynching), was hardly

Observing a great herd of buffalo in *Dances with Wolves* (1990), starring Kevin Costner, Graham Greene, Rodney A. Grant, Mary McDonnell, courtesy Photofest

"a time when the color of a person's skin was unimportant." But she's not really talking about the historic West. She's talking about our idealized West, and in that sense she's right, color *doesn't* matter—individuals are judged according to their skills and their character. That's one of the reasons we love the *idea* of the frontier so much!

Though we might bemoan this romanticization—and a strong argument can be made for the way stereotypic and simplistic representations have devalued entire groups of people—the fact remains this ideal inspires a highly *diverse* audience. For Western fans, regardless of their backgrounds, it represents the best of what we are, the best of what we can be. It is an era many want to be a part of, some vicariously, others literally—an expression of their own lives, characters, capabilities, desires, and choices.

> *I feel sad that I missed this era of our nation's history. Sometimes I feel I was born too late. I like adventure. I like the thought of riding over country that no white man or woman has ever seen before, land untouched by civilization, uncluttered. I understand why the Indians fought so hard to save it. That's why I chose to write Western novels—I wanted, somehow, some way, to be a part of that time. Granted, it's a small part, but it satisfies some of the longing.*
>
> Novelist, 33, white man, Texas

And not only are they inspired by the frontier spirit, but many Western fans report that watching their favorite Westerns gives them a sense of well-being. They identify with events and characters on the screen in ways that validate their beliefs, perspectives, and choices.

> *Westerns give me the feeling of strength and power achieved after reaching the bottom and truly searching your soul, and still triumphing over deceit and selfishness.*
>
> Carpenter/mason/artist, 49, white man, California

Watching their favorite Westerns, many say, can alleviate stress, can even make them feel rejuvenated, ready to stand up for what they believe in, to persevere.

Sometimes I watch a Western after working a very emotional and

I have always felt like I should have been born and raised out West. I love the outdoors, with its uncrowded vast and rugged beauty. I love the solitude that it brings where you can stand and look out and imagine what it was like 150 years ago when 60 million buffalo roamed the prairie and Native Americans roamed and lived off the land unspoiled by man, in its natural state.

> Supermarket manager, 65, white man, Tennessee

A good Western makes me feel ambitious. After I see a film that I really enjoy, I feel I can do anything. I feel that I could achieve any goals. It makes me feel powerful.

> Salesclerk, 33, white woman, Wyoming

When I was a kid, I loved Westerns because here was the life I wanted to live. When I grew up, I went west (now live in Alaska) and lived that life—working on ranches. I feel hemmed in in cities or places with mega people. Westerns give me room. They relax me and make me feel I've come home. The good guys win and the bad get their just deserts. It's usually easy to tell which side is which, so my sense of justice is appeased.

> Teacher/writer/homemaker, 64, white woman, New England

Westerns give me pride and a sense of power when standing up for something you believe in.

> Security manager for a large retailer, 37, white woman, California

I love Westerns because it is a romanticized ideal of what life was like 100 (150-200) years ago. And I feel that I was born a century too late. I spent my formative years being a loner and spending most of my time in the woods, learning how to be quiet in movement, what plants were edible, and how to talk to a superior being (God, if you must). I learned how to be comfortable alone, the feeling of oneness with nature. And how terrified unknown noises, smells, etc., can make one feel.

> Small business co-owner, 60, white woman, New York

Westerns seem to give you a good feeling of getting something done.

> Stunt actor/rancher, 72, white man, Texas

Westerns make me feel good. They give me something to shoot for in my own life. They give me a place to escape to. They help me to see the good things I have and the bad things I can get rid of in my life. They give me someone to cheer on and root for. They help me to think about a past that has principles that should and can be carried to the present and future.

Disabled, 58, white woman, Colorado

I feel that whatever dreams I have can come true with a little hard work. And just the way these settlers made big changes in their lives, I feel sometimes that's what you have to do in order to reach your goal. These people all had "Grit"!

Hotel front desk agent, 57, Latino woman, New York

I'm supposed to be seen as a good guy. I don't carry a gun. My whole job is to help people. Yet in my 12 years in Emergency Medical Services, I've been robbed of my drug box, shot at, threatened with knives, broken glass, fists, spit on, and sworn at by people I was trying to help, their friends and relatives, and total strangers. Watching the old Westerns helps me to recharge my belief in ultimate justice and the goodness that can exist in the human race.

Paramedic, 52, white man, Iowa

stressful shift at work, simply to reaffirm that the values I have were once appreciated by my country. Too often today, we daily must confront individuals at our workplaces (both customers and employees) who seem to have very low moral codes or an objectionable set of manners. With the rigid requirements of today's business culture, we cannot simply look these folks in the eye and tell them to go to Hell. The Westerns (romanticized, yes) reflect a time of "black and white" honor, responsibility, and morality; and I feel better about myself and my job after watching them.

Retail salesman, 57, white man, Minnesota

Watching a Western restores my beliefs in what's right or wrong. It gives me a pat on the back and rushes me back into the fight. It tells me that the truths I held as a young man are still valid and worth

From left to right, Charlie Sheen, Dermot Mulroney, Kiefer Sutherland, Emilio Estevez, Casey Siemaszko, and Lou Diamond Phillips in *Young Guns* (1988), courtesy Photofest

keeping. It supports me and tells me that I am not the only one who believes and holds these truths. It reminds me to be true to myself.

Salesman, 53, Latino man, Colorado

Clearly, the frontier spirit continues to energize us—and though there aren't many new Westerns made, successful ones from the past 20 years (*Silverado, Young Guns, Dances with Wolves, Lonesome Dove, Unforgiven, Tombstone*) show that the genre still offers audiences fresh looks at a familiar and treasured myth that can give us hope and inspiration. It can empower us to keep going, to strive for more, to believe people can be good, to fantasize, to dream, to imagine.

When life stresses get too hard, I can see through the eyes of Old West characters and handle things much better. Be it outlaws, lawmen, or whatever reminds me of me or the way I wish to be.

Professional driver, 49, white man, New Jersey

Westerns take us out of our everyday lives, away from our responsibilities.

I want to be alone and get away from everyone and everything, and just ride away into the sunset.

Retired secretary, 75, white woman

They give us a vision of relationships between men and women that is uncomplicated, with gender roles clearly defined.

I feel more at home during those time periods. Life seemed so much simpler than now. You didn't have drugs. Women could be home with their kids and the men had to worry about finances. Sometimes I wish I could live in those times.

Therapy aide, 48, white woman, New York

They liberate us from social constraints, material possessions, and what often seem to be arbitrary and inane restrictions imposed by zoning boards, school districts, employers, government bureaucracy.

They don't have to deal with today's rules and regulations to get something done. Truly another time.

Store manager, 63, white man, California

Watching a Western brings up emotions of sadness, anger, joy, fear, relief after conflicts have been settled, laughter, feeling good, strong and more powerful, and a sense of belonging. Not being alone to solve problems.

Musician/entertainer, 46, white man, Massachusetts

I feel a strong connection to a character when I see him or her make the same decision as I would. It makes me feel right.

Teacher, 36, white woman, Rhode Island

If it's a "good" Western—well-acted, with a good story—it makes for fine entertainment. Then it gives me a "lift," makes me proud to be an American. The story of the pioneers of the Old West is, I think, unique in the annals of Western civilization. These people had the guts to conquer a continent.

Retired secretary, 82, white woman, New York

I love Westerns because they reflect a time when people had the opportunity to decide how they wanted to live; they deal with issues of right and wrong with less need for political niceties, and they often depict the harm political niceties can inflict. They deal with people who create their lives in a wild, open land—and they deal with the conflicts in that wild open land.

CNN copy editor, 49, white woman, Kentucky

They are a window back to a simpler time when this country was young and untamed and unspoiled, and the people were untamed and unspoiled, too. By that I mean they were naive to the manufactured stresses of life and they were faced with far fewer choices. Their lives were full of adventure!

Title III program director, 47, white woman, Illinois

Westerns bring up disgust with the modern world as one by one we are forced to conform to what is conceived as the "right" thing. You cannot discipline your child without someone sticking their beliefs in it (e.g., the woman who slapped her child in the supermarket). You must build your home "just so" to fit the community ideal. You must mow your lawn as often as your neighbor. You must have permission to build, remodel, or do anything on your own land.

Homemaker, 60, white woman, New York

The characters are usually courageous and possess an incredible sense of freedom. I would love to just pick myself up and go (anywhere), but I am so tied down with my job, social obligations, political obligations, and personal obligations, and in addition possessions (that now possess me).

Accountant, 39, white woman, New York

Westerns may not be true to the nuances and complexity of the history of the Old West, but they strip away the conveniences of modern life and give us the opportunity to experience, however vicariously, what it might have taken to survive on the frontier when you had only yourself or a small community to rely on. They tap into deep longings for a time gone by and offer escape from daily responsibilities and social constraints, appealing to and stimulating our imaginations with their idealized vision of a frontier spirit. In our fast-paced world of stress and tight schedules, Westerns offer fans a chance to relax, take a breath, revitalize, and jump back into the fray of modern life.

John Wayne and Montgomery Clift bond after a fistfight in *Red River* (1948), courtesy Photofest.

CHAPTER 3

Growing Up Western

If you love Westerns today, it's probably been a lifelong passion; few people have discovered the genre as adults (although it has been known to happen). Most fans who love Westerns today grew up loving the Old West of the silver and/or small screen. And this really isn't surprising. From the 1930s through the early 1970s, Westerns were a staple of popular entertainment. With big-budget Westerns to Bs and serials to weekly television shows, Americans lived off a pop culture diet of beans and hay for 40 years. And while early on you may have had to wait Saturday to Saturday to get your sagebrush fix, once television hit the scene, you could tune in to watch your favorite cowboys every day of the week. Even today, Westerns from that era are readily available on cable television or via videotape/DVD to all generations of Western fans.

Theater interior with poster announcing an appearance by Roy Rogers, c. early 1940s, courtesy Photofest

From early childhood, I watched Roy Rogers on TV; I was hooked. When I watch Westerns, I relive my childhood with the freedom to roam as a cowboy, no obligations, and tomorrow bringing new adventure!

Store clerk, 51, white man, Virginia

My love of Westerns goes back to listening to The Lone Ranger on the radio! Always played Cowboys and Indians (with or without the horse)!

Bank manager, 61, white woman, Colorado

I grew up every Saturday at the movie matinee, reading Western stories, playing Cowboys and Indians, working on my grandparents' farm and ranch. My dad and uncle were cowboys, going to and participating in rodeos, cattle work.

Teacher, 62, white man, Texas

At an early age (eight), I was taken to see a cowboy film starring George O'Brien—taken by an aunt—and to this day, I can see myself engrossed in watching that film. I've followed Western movies to this day and am familiar with almost all the movie cowboys.

Retired businessman, 80, white man, Connecticut

As a child, I always played cowboys. Made a saddle of rugs for my father's sawhorse. Liked all the cowboy songs.

Retired, 80, white man, Pennsylvania

I think my boyhood of playing cowboy (even a horseless cowboy) had a lot to do with my love of the Western. My wife always told me that I would have been a very handsome cowboy (flattery got her everywhere)!

Retired from the U.S. Army Post of Engineers, 79, white man, Kansas

B Westerns are just my favorite. Movies with Tonto and the Lone Ranger are great.

Grocery store owner, 66, Native American man, Virginia

As a child, my brother and I attended Western movies every Saturday (almost). After the movies, we would go home and act out the roles that we had just seen. It was great fun.

Maintenance supervisor, 67, white man, Ohio

I have a happy remembrance of going to the Saturday movies and then going home to strap on my cap guns to play cowboy (if I didn't wear them to the theater, which was a neighborhood theater that I walked to). Just seeing Roy Rogers on the screen and knowing what a great person he was gives me a warm feeling.

Attorney, 59, white man, Ohio

Watching my favorite Westerns, Young Guns I and II, brings back happy memories of when I used to play guns with my brothers.

Dishwasher, 46, white man, Colorado

Of course, movie Westerns were long established as a favored American genre by 1930 through silent pictures. In fact, early Westerns were shot shortly after the frontier "closed" (1890-1910) and many former frontiersmen (cowpunchers, sharpshooters, lawmen, Indians, even ex-outlaws), some of whom had turned initially to the Wild West Shows, went to Hollywood and signed on as actors, writers, directors, and consultants. They helped shape what had often been a harsh and cruel way of life into an idealized—but believable—past. Former outlaw Al Jennings, for example, directed a reenactment of his own holdup in 1908's *The Bank Robbery*. Better known westerners Bat Masterson and Wyatt Earp also served as consultants in Hollywood's renditions of their own exploits. Silent-era cowboy star Tom Mix himself was a former horse handler, cowboy, rodeo competitor, and lawman.

But for most of today's fans, it was the Western movies, serials, and TV shows made from the 1930s to the early 1970s that captured their imaginations. As children, they joined in countless adventures riding the range, cheering the good guys and booing the bad. They filled movie theaters or living rooms and, once the onscreen action was done, played Cowboys and Indians in countless reenactments of their favorite adventures on imaginary horses. It was a cultural phenomenon; millions of boys and girls, from such different backgrounds that many had little in common, were swept up in the excitement and lured by the freedom of the open range.

Wyatt Earp, date unknown, courtesy Buffalo Bill Historical Center, Cody, Wyoming; Vincent Mercaldo Collection; P.71.2059.1

> *I love the action, the horses, the great scenery, the good versus the bad, the firearms, the history, and the strong individual characters. Since I was a young boy, I have been captivated by cowboys and Westerns. They were, to me, the gateway to adventure and excitement!*
>
> Gas utility construction foreman, 53, white man, Minnesota

That the Western achieved such enormous popularity during these decades (1930-1970) is actually somewhat surprising—the genre was struggling at the end of the 1920s. In fact, *New Yorker* film critic Paulene Kael may have declared the Western dead in 1974 ("A few more Westerns may straggle in, but the Western is dead"), but popular fan magazine *Photoplay* signaled the end of the genre much earlier—*in 1929*. In words foreshadowing Kael's remarks, editor James Quirk noted, "Lindbergh has put the cowboy into the discard as a type of national hero. The Western novel and motion picture heroes have slunk away into the brush, never to return."

Big-budget Western production had waned somewhat in the late 1920s, audiences responding poorly to epic tales of the Wild West. Western filmmakers were also struggling to adjust to one of the biggest changes ever to hit the film industry—the transition to sound. While films featuring dialogue and music transitioned quite well, early sound technology did not lend itself well to outdoor settings; cumbersome equipment couldn't be moved, placing a premium on dialogue over action or epic reenactment. In addition, small-town movie theaters, where Westerns were especially popular, were the last to be wired for sound.

As a result of these trends, few larger budget Westerns were released in the transition years, particularly 1929 to 1931, and those with uneven results. *In Old Arizona* and *The Virginian* (both in 1929) were box office successes and demonstrated sound could effectively be used in Westerns, capturing the rumble of galloping horses and the crack of gunshots. The grand-scale epic *Cimarron* (1931) was also a top-grossing film for that year, winning the Academy Award for best picture, a feat unmatched by any Western until *Dances with Wolves* in 1990. Even so, however, it lost money in Depression-era America. And what should have been a box office smash, *The Big Trail* (1930), directed by *In Old Arizona's* Raoul Walsh and starring a young John Wayne, was a dismal failure. This was primarily because the movie was filmed in wide-screen and exhibitors who had just invested in sound equipment were unwilling and unable to invest in the additional technology needed to show wide-screen movies. Nonetheless, studios were leery of sinking large amounts of cash into a genre that wasn't proving itself steadily at the box office—a view reinforced when Westerns crafted by the likes of Cecil B. DeMille also floundered.

But parallel to the production of A (for "A quality" or "adult") Westerns throughout this period was that of lower budget B (for "budget" or "B quality") one to five reel movies and serials. Made for $110,000

Opposite top, from left to right, Walter Huston and Gary Cooper, *The Virginian* (1929), courtesy Photofest

Opposite bottom, from left to right, Richard Dix, William Collier Jr., Irene Dunne, *Cimarron* (1931), courtesy Photofest

John Wayne as Breck Coleman, *The Big Trail* (1930), courtesy Photofest

William S. Hart, publicity shot c. 1930, courtesy Photofest

or less (compared, for example, to the $782,000 budget for 1923's 10-reel box office success, *The Covered Wagon*), these Westerns were highly formulaic and quickly churned out, filmed in just a few weeks. They featured easily recognizable heroes and villains and prioritized chases, fist-fights, daredevil feats, and shootouts over epic scope, complex characterization, or social commentary. Their most successful incarnation was Tom Mix. Foregoing the realism his contemporary William S. Hart strove for, Mix's commercialized and fanciful cowboy didn't smoke, drink, or kill—in fact, he preferred subduing his villains using elaborate lasso-work or stunts rather than gunplay. Tom Mix was so popular that, at the height of his career in the 1920s, children's letters to his horse Tony just needed to be addressed to "Tony, California" to find their way to the Mix ranch.

Sound familiar? Indeed, Tom Mix set the stage for the B Western heroes of the 1930s through the early 1950s. Gene Autry's Cowboy Code, sometimes referred to as the Cowboy Commandments, could easily have applied to Tom Mix, where, in essence: A cowboy shoots only when shot at; is true to his word; treats women, children, the elderly, and animals with respect; comes to the aid of people in need; rises above religious and racial intolerance; keeps himself above reproach in all ways.

With the A Western struggling, the Western transitioned into Depression-era America primarily through its B and serial forms. People were staying home, unwilling to spend limited cash during tough times on just two hours or so worth of entertainment. As a consequence, studios were losing millions—Fox, RKO, and Paramount were nearly bankrupt in 1932. To bring audiences back to movie houses, exhibitors and studios had to be creative. Exhibitors, for example, started offering gimmicks—free groceries, dishes, ticket stub giveaway games. Screeno, a version of bingo or Keno, was a big draw. One night a week was known as "Bank Night" and the audience would get free Screeno cards with their movie tickets and could win cash or prizes.

> *My love for Westerns started as a child when my family went to the old serial movies every Saturday night at the old uptown theater on Fredericksburg Road. They had a drawing for free groceries.*
>
> Retired bookkeeper, 83, white woman, Texas

But the most compelling bargain of all was the double feature—the A and B movies featured on a double bill—which caught on, especially in neighborhood and small-town theaters. And what better format for the second feature than the already proven B Western, which was usually just 50 to 70 minutes long, and, by the 1930s, made for as little as $5,000—John Wayne filmed B Westerns in this period in as little as three days.

Tom Mix, publicity shot c. 1925, courtesy Photofest

I spent my formative years Saturdays at the movies to see COWBOY movies and serials! Brings back happy memories of my childhood and the enjoyment playing cowboys with my friends. They were very good days, even though it was the Depression. Took away any cares that we might have had.

Retired inspector, 82, white man, New York

I always wanted to be a cowboy when I was a boy—not a sports hero or doctor or lawyer. When I see an old Western, I think of my youth and my dad who I would go with and cheer for the good guy and sing along with Gene and Roy and punch the bad guy like Duke did!

Chemical handler, 61, white man, New Jersey

As a youth right after the Depression, all we could afford was the movie on Saturday night. These old movies bring back those times when nine of us children filed into an old Chevrolet and rode eight miles over dirt roads to the movies. It was a simple time when we were poor, but happy.

Retired from the military, 74, white man, North Carolina

We used to attend to boo the villain and throw popcorn! FUN!!

Retired elementary school teacher, 71, white woman, Ohio

I grew up on them. In the '50s, John Wayne, James Stewart, Alan Ladd as Shane. These were my heroes. Every Saturday and Sunday, my friends and I attended the movies for hours. For 50 cents, we got two features, newsreels, 21 cartoons, coming attractions. It was great!

Dressmaker, 60, black woman, Kentucky

There was only one movie theater in town. Every Friday and Saturday night, it showed a Western and a more modern movie. My father took me every Friday night. My father loved Westerns. Those heroes were Roy Rogers, Johnny Mack Brown, Rod Cameron, Bob Steele, Gabby Hayes, and Gene Autry. We never missed a Lone Ranger on the radio. I loved the horses and the idea that there was a hero to make things right, take care of the "bad guys"!

Retired bookkeeper, 71, white woman, Illinois

During the Depression years, Westerns were an inexpensive escape from contemporary problems. As morality plays, they emphasized civic virtues. As youngsters, we identified with the heroes—Wild Bill Elliott, Gene Autry, Roy Rogers, Allan "Rocky" Lane, Johnny Mack Brown, and Tex Ritter. No matter how bleak the plot was by the second reel, we knew things would turn out well at the end.

Retired history professor, 70, Latino man, Texas

Lash LaRue series are my favorites. The directness of Lash's persona—he did many of his own stunts. Realism in that you saw him reload. Most of all, the whip action! Action, drastic action is taken, and Victory!

Salvation Army officer, 64, white man, Mississippi

Watching Western movies with Hoppy, Gene, and Roy brings back many memories of Saturdays at the Liberty and Allen theatres. Yes, I would go to two theatres on Saturday, see four Westerns, two serial chapters, and two cartoons. From age four to age 17 was a very happy time in my life. I looked forward from Saturday to Saturday to see my favorite cowboy stars.

Retired insurance agency vice president, 68, white man, North Carolina

As with their silent screen predecessors, Depression-era B Westerns were highly formulaic and stressed action over plot. Better-known studios such as RKO, Columbia, and Universal released Bs, but it was the independent, "Poverty Row" studios such as Tiffany, Puritan, Mascot, and, most notably, Republic, that made the genre famous with the likes of Gene Autry, Roy Rogers, Hopalong Cassidy, Ken Maynard, Lash LaRue, Allan "Rocky" Lane, Sunset Carson, and Johnny Mack Brown. Parables of teamwork, helping your neighbor, thwarting evil bankers, all showing that the American character would win out over hard times—these were very popular to audiences in the 1930s and into the 1940s. And it was these Bs and serials that captured the imagination of a new generation of Western fans, creating such a strong bond, such familiarity, that cowboy stars became like their friends. In fact, many fans refer to their favorite Western stars by their first names.

It helps me to remember those years when I dreamed of riding in a posse with Roy and the "group." One thing I recall is the intense "high" I felt upon leaving the theater—I couldn't wait to get home and get into my cowboy outfit and ride my imaginary horse—particularly after a Roy Rogers or Rocky Lane picture.

Newspaper advertising sales rep, 60, white man, New Hampshire

Life was—or appeared—less complicated. We always knew that goodness would win in the end—that feeling inspired confidence, especially as the financial situation was not good. The older "B" Westerns were as friends, for one knew the cowboy and could relate to him.

Retired businessman, 80, white man, Connecticut

These B Western idols filled movie palaces from the 1930s through

Roy Rogers and Trigger greeting fans, c. mid-1940s, used by permission of The Roy Rogers-Dale Evans Museum

the early 1950s, kept children glued to television sets in the 1950s, and helped line many corporate pockets (inside Hollywood and out) from the 1930s through the 1950s. Wherever they appeared, particularly Gene Autry, Roy Rogers and Dale Evans, and William Boyd (Hopalong Cassidy), crowds filled parade routes, concert halls, amphitheaters, and stadiums. Children begged their parents for six-guns, holsters, outfits, hats, watches, milk glasses, cereal bowls, comic books, and a host of other tie-ins featuring their favorite cowboy stars. In the fifty years that have passed since they filled our screens (both large and small), in the wake of the tremendously successful A Westerns of the 1950s and 1960s, and in the shadow of John Wayne and Clint Eastwood, it is easy to forget just how popular these B Western stars were.

On the advice of humorist Will Rogers, Gene Autry pursued a career in entertainment, starting on the radio in 1928 and scoring a hit record by 1931. Within three years, he was doing film work, appearing in Ken Maynard's *In Old Santa Fe* (1934). Autry was chosen to star in Republic's 1935 off-beat serial, *The Phantom Empire,* and, by 1937, he was America's

I love the singing cowboy Western—I didn't like the John Wayne type—rough language and degrading women. Gene Autry made me feel there were some men who could bring law and order, plus be kind and respectful of women. He had a sense of humor, a beautiful singing voice, and always stood for justice. I guess I'm a romantic. I loved the scenery, the music, the humor, and Gene riding Champion! And best of all—Gene would get the girl without a lot of the sickening mush you see portrayed in movies today!!

Retired schoolteacher, 78, white woman, Kansas

All Gene Autry movies—they were exciting—had lots of action, lots of horses—no sex scenes—lots of good music. Hero, horse, music, nature, scenery, and action. I like the sound of the horses' hooves. Hearing Roy Rogers and Dale Evans sing—ahh, bliss!

Retired teacher, 67, white woman, Colorado

I was raised in the country. I used to go to movies on weekends and watch Gene Autry and Roy Rogers. We liked to watch the cowboys with the horses.

Retired social services case aide, 65, black woman, Texas

Favorite Cowboy. Always finding time to break into song between action sequences, Gene Autry charmed audiences with his easy manner, moral credo, and one-two punch. With Champion, "Wonder Horse of the West," and sidekicks Smiley Burnett, then Pat Buttram, he appeared in 93 feature films and 91 episodes of *The Gene Autry Show*. Of the 635 songs he recorded, he wrote or co-wrote 300, including his signature "Back in the Saddle Again." "Rudolph the Red-Nosed Reindeer," one of his greatest hits, is the second most popular Christmas recording of all time (behind Bing Crosby's "White Christmas").

Though Gene Autry was America's first singing cowboy superstar, this was only one of his many accomplishments. He was the first to have a certified gold record (1931's "That Silver-Haired Daddy of Mine"), the first performer to sell out Madison Square Garden, the first country musician to be awarded a star on the Hollywood Walk of Fame, and the first (and only) celebrity to have a total of five such stars (one each for radio, records, movies, television, and live performances). In the early 1950s, he purchased his movies and put them on television, which helped him amass a great fortune he parlayed into broadcast station ownership

Gene Autry stopping traffic on one of Philadelphia's busiest downtown streets, c. late 1940s, courtesy Photofest

Roy Rogers and Dale Evans movies are my favorites. Good wins out over evil, the cowboy gets the girl, they ride off into the sunset. What could be simpler? As children, we needed "heroes"—these were and continue to be mine.

Advertising agency office manager, 55, white woman, Virginia

Roy Rogers the singing cowboy was my favorite because every Saturday morning, when you were a kid, you had something to look forward to and not be out in the street, when you could watch Roy and Trigger. When I watch my favorite Western, it makes me think about when my mother was alive, because we used to watch TV all the time on Saturday/Sunday. We used to have such a good time watching Westerns.

Security guard, 52, black man, Louisiana

and, his great love, ownership of the California Angels baseball team. Gene Autry died in 1998 at the age of 91, having spent 70 years in the entertainment industry.

During World War II, Gene Autry served as a sergeant in the Army Air Corps, ferrying fuel, ammunition, and arms in China, Burma, and India. After the war, he toured with the USO in the South Pacific before returning to Hollywood in 1946. In the interim, another singing cowboy came to the fore. He was born Leonard Slye, but, by the late 1930s, was better known by his stage name, Roy Rogers. Appearing in his first Republic Western in 1938, *Under Western Stars*, the studio dubbed Rogers "King of the Cowboys" in Gene Autry's absence, a title that still stands today. Boyish and athletic, with a wonderfully rich singing voice, Roy Rogers never lost his youthful love for adventure. He performed many of his own stunts and perfected his marksmanship (and artistry) with all manner of weapons (handgun, rifle, shotgun, bow and arrow, even a slingshot, which he taught his young viewers to make). He was a rancher, horse breeder and trainer, as well as an outdoors enthusiast, a hunter and fisherman. He loved to bowl, enjoyed golfing, but always had a flair for fast and dangerous sports—motorcycle riding, speedboat racing.

Roy Rogers starred in 88 films, 28 with Dale Evans, Queen of the West, before they moved their show to television in 1951. Always a dash of romance (but never too mushy—he never kissed Dale on screen, though he did kiss his horse Trigger), a Roy Rogers/Dale Evans movie guaranteed action, great horsemanship (Trigger, "the smartest horse in the movies," reputedly had a repertoire of over 70 tricks, including untying knots and shooting a gun), and a satisfying, happy ending. When it came to foiling dastardly plots, no one did it better than Roy and Dale.

Off the set, the Rogers (Roy and Dale were married off-screen) de-

Gene Autry in uniform, 1943, courtesy Photofest

Roy Rogers rears Trigger, c. 1950-1953, used by permission of The Roy Rogers-Dale Evans Museum

voted themselves to children's organizations, adopting four children and fostering one themselves, and founding the Happy Trails Children's Foundation for abused and neglected children. No stranger to tragedy, Roy Rogers' first wife, Arline, died one week after his son Roy Jr. was born. He and Dale subsequently buried three of their nine children. But that didn't stop them from carrying on their public lives. Roy Rogers frequently greeted and interacted with fans at his museum, right up until his death in 1998. He was 86.

William Boyd, or Hopalong Cassidy as he came to be known, achieved B Western stardom through a different route. Never the youthful, singing cowboy, Boyd was an older actor and prematurely gray. Born in Ohio, he grew up in Oklahoma and came to Hollywood in 1918, eventually landing work as a leading man for director Cecil B. DeMille. As a silent-screen star throughout the 1920s, he had a reputation as a partier, drinker, and womanizer. In fact, he was married and divorced three times before marrying actress Grace Bradley, a union that would last 35 years.

In the mid-1930s, a Paramount Pictures producer, Harry "Pop"

Trigger kisses Roy Rogers, 1939, used by permission of The Roy Rogers-Dale Evans Museum

Sherman, convinced the studio to produce a series of Westerns based on the Hopalong Cassidy novels and short stories written by Clarence E. Mulford. Boyd landed the role in 1935, and, in his late 30s, became Hopalong Cassidy. The role seemed to transform the man as the man transformed the role. As originally crafted, Hopalong Cassidy was a hard-drinking, hard-tempered, hard-talkin' but straight-shootin' cowhand. Under Boyd's adaptation, however, Hopalong became a paragon of virtue—wholesome, kind, very much a father figure to young fans, and with a signature laugh that entertained audiences worldwide. With his horse Topper and sidekicks, who included Andy Clyde, Russell Hayden, and George "Gabby" Hayes, Boyd created a model B Western world of eternal optimism, confidence, and virtue. Boyd extended the Hoppy persona off-screen, making thousands of appearances to often tens, if not *hundreds of thousands* of people, always striving to represent the Hoppy image in every way possible. True to Hoppy's creed for fairness, for example, Boyd refused to make a scheduled appearance at a department store in Atlanta in 1950 because the children were segregated into two lines—one for "coloreds" and one for whites. Only when the store agreed to integrate the

William Boyd, studio portrait, c. mid-1920s, courtesy Photofest

William Boyd as Hopalong Cassidy, c. 1940, courtesy Photofest

William Boyd as Hopalong Cassidy appearing to over 60,000 in Des Moines, Iowa, 1950, courtesy Photofest

At the age of 10, the Newark, N.J. channel had a Western film show hosted by Tex Ritter. It was on every day with films starring Ken Maynard, Bob Steele, their groups "The Range Busters" and "The Rough Riders," Hopalong Cassidy, et al. Westerns were an escape to a free environment, without anyone telling you what to do!

Retired controller's assistant, 65, white man, New Jersey

High on the list is any movie with the Sons of the Pioneers in it, Hopalong Cassidy, Gene Autry, Johnny Mack Brown, John Wayne (1930–1940), The Three Mesquiteers, The Lone Ranger serial. I like the story, outdoor scenes, music. The "bad guys" are always caught; hero has ethics to look up to; Western songs make me feel good!

Retired aircraft design engineer, 77, white man, Oklahoma

Hopalong Cassidy was a role model for young people, espousing high morals. His movies recall a happier, less stressful part of my life.

Retired radio and TV marketer, 70, white woman

lines did Boyd agree to appear. Though his actions went unrecognized—the local paper reported that the children met their cowboy hero in two lines—this insistence on fairness and decency permeated Boyd's actions.

In the mid-1940s, Boyd realized what a phenomenon Hopalong Cassidy had become and, taking a gamble, sold most everything he owned to purchase all rights to the Hopalong Cassidy films and name. Releasing the films to television (as Gene Autry and Roy Rogers would subsequently do with their pictures) was only his initial step, however. By the early 1950s, over 100 manufacturers were offering Hopalong Cassidy products. Stores were full of Hopalong Cassidy outfits, six-guns, holsters, lunch boxes, toys, glasses, cereal bowls, comic books—2,500 different items at the height of Hoppy's popularity. And Boyd selected Hoppy merchandise personally and carefully—he would never endorse bubblegum, for example, because he didn't approve of it.

There were certainly precedents for leveraging such merchandising opportunities—in the 1920s, you could easily find Tom Mix guns and holsters, decoding badges, rings, belts, pins, picture frames, glasses, and plates. But William Boyd was the first to take it to such a large scale (and Gene Autry and Roy Rogers soon followed suit). After 66 Hoppy films, plus 52 half-hour shows for NBC (only 12 were pared down from his films), and thousands of personal appearances worldwide, William Boyd retired in the mid-1950s. He died of congestive heart failure and Parkinson's in 1972 at age 74.

By the mid-1950s, the B Western was transitioning to a burgeoning new medium—television. When William Boyd retired, he was concerned about his production company, particularly the people who would be put out of work. CBS was beginning to shoot a new Western, however, so Boyd turned his company over to the network. That Western, starring a young, relatively unknown actor named James Arness, would run for 20 years. *Gunsmoke* was the first adult Western on television and tackled many sensitive issues of its day, including civil rights, social protest, child abuse, even rape.

> *Gunsmoke's writers managed to provide (show after show) an interesting and exciting (but believable) account of an experience focusing intensely on one or more basic areas of life. It is admirable that each episode contained valuable idealistic moral(s) which have been for so long esteemed most highly by responsible American people.*
>
> Retired mortgage company president, 69, white man, Mississippi

But *Gunsmoke* was hardly the only choice available on television. Throughout its 20-year run, viewers could tune in every night of the week to favorite sagebrush sagas, including *The Lone Ranger, Maverick, Rawhide,*

> *I grew up with Gunsmoke reruns and the Cowboy thing. I've always been a "Cowboy," and it's been intensified since I started Cowboy Action Shooting.*
>
> Entrepreneur, 31, white man, North Carolina

Hopalong Cassidy merchandise, courtesy
Harry Rinker and U.S. Television Office, Inc.

The Lawman, Colt .45, Tales of Wells Fargo, Cheyenne, The Life and Legend of Wyatt Earp, The Rifleman, Wagon Train, Laramie, Wanted: Dead or Alive, Dick Powell's Zane Grey Theatre, Bat Masterson, Zorro, Have Gun Will Travel, The Virginian, Daniel Boone, Laredo, Cimarron Strip, Bonanza, The Wild Wild West, High Chaparral, Big Valley, and many more—some lasting just a few episodes. For many fans, it was the Westerns on television, not those in the movie theaters, that brought them to the genre.

Much of my earliest exposure to the idea of right and wrong came from watching My Pal Trigger *and similar morality plays on television. There was no confusion about who was the hero and who was the villain like in modern movies. And I could look out the window and see cars and trucks on the road just like on the screen. I thought*

*I grew up watching Westerns on TV (*Gunsmoke, Rawhide, Bonanza, Roy Rogers, The Lone Ranger, *etc.). My parents were always very selective in what we all watched, but Westerns were never questioned. Most even had a moral value to them. The Old West has always intrigued me—it had a romance about it—maybe because I lived in town. Any Western on the "silver screen" was honest and decent then, and most are today (if they are real Westerns). The scenery in most Westerns is beautiful—different from my everyday, and there is always a hero. I love heroes!*

Bookkeeper, 54, white woman, Mississippi

*Westerns bring back happy and secure memories of my childhood—my friends and I had a great time playing Cowboys(girls) and Indians. Annie Oakley was my heroine. I remember TV shows the most as I saw them most often (*Annie O., The Lone Ranger, Roy Rogers/Dale Evans, *and later* Wagon Train, Maverick, Bonanza). *As a kid, my fantasy world featured me as a superhero-cowgirl-type character who would ride onto the scene on my trusty steed and go about "righting wrongs" or rescuing loved ones in distress.*

Registered nurse, 57, white woman, Massachusetts

From left to right, James Arness, Amanda Blake, Milburn Stone, and Dennis Weaver of *Gunsmoke,* c. 1960, courtesy Photofest

Clockwise from top right, Clint Walker as Cheyenne Bodie in *Cheyenne* (1955-1963); Chuck Connors as Lucas McCain in *The Rifleman* (1958-1963); The cast of *The High Chaparral* (1968-1971) clockwise Leif Erickson, Henry Darrow, Mark Slade, Linda Cristal, Cameron Mitchell (1967-1971); Clayton Moore in the title role, *The Lone Ranger* (1949-1957); James Garner as Bret Maverick in *Maverick* (1957-1962); and the cast of *The Big Valley* (1965-1969) clockwise from left, Lee Majors, Peter Breck, Richard Long, Barbara Stanwyck, and Linda Evans. Center photo, Fess Parker in the title role, *Daniel Boone* (1964-1970). All photos courtesy Photofest.

what I was seeing was real, and I sure wanted to be like Roy Rogers, not to mention the Lone Ranger, the Cisco Kid, etc. I guess I sort of become that innocent child again when I watch those shows. The Lone Ranger, Bonanza, Gunsmoke, and other TV Westerns in some ways are more important to how I feel about Westerns than the movies.

Paramedic, 52, white man, Iowa

Throughout the 1950s and 1960s, Hollywood continued to produce large budget Westerns for theatrical release while television took up the mantle of the B Western and mesmerized an entirely new generation of fans. This widespread availability of Westerns on both the large and small screens gave the genre a dominance in popular culture not seen before or since. There were Westerns for everybody, all ages, all members of the family. In fact, watching and enjoying Westerns was a cross-generational experience, one that parents, children, and extended families shared (and *had* shared, really, since the early 1900s, when the genre in its cinematic form had begun to so capture the American imagination).

As today's fans think about why they love Westerns, one of the themes emerging repeatedly is this very issue of a family connection. In particular, fans talk about spending time with siblings and parents (especially fathers); piling into a car and riding down a dirt road to the only theater in town, taking younger siblings to the movies to give mom a break for the afternoon, singing songs together, or spending time watching Westerns with a now-deceased parent.

Reminds me of my dad and my wonderful youth.

Trucker, Latino man, California

I grew up with my family learning about my cultures, listening to and singing country music, and watching any Western available.

Lab technician, 47, Native American man, Rhode Island

Watching my favorite Western brings up a certain amount of security. My dad died when I was 17, but we always used to go to Saturday night at the movies, mom, dad, and I. I always loved those times.

Hair stylist, 55, white woman, Massachusetts

Westerns bring back happy memories of times I spent watching TV with my parents when I was young.

Librarian, 50, white woman, California

Reminds me of good times growing up with my father.

Flooring contractor, 57, white man, California

Watching a good Western has always been like going home for me. I was raised in a family of "Western addicts." This common love bridged both the generation gap and also the gap between the sexes.

Elementary school teacher, 61, white woman, Iowa

My dad always loved the West. I think because of him, I did, too.

Retired schoolteacher, 78, white woman, Illinois

My dad was a huge Western fan. He grew up watching Randolph Scott, Alan Ladd, Gary Cooper, and John Wayne. I fell right in line and loved them even more! I grew up watching John Wayne, Clint Eastwood, Henry Fonda, and others. I guess it's the action, the rugged locations, maybe the power of life and death with a Colt .45 on your hip. The West was wide open, the dream of the unknown. Being out in the great outdoors. I guess it's mainly being a kid again.

Butcher, 43, white man, Georgia

It reminds me of the setting of watching them as a kid. My dad is dead now, and I enjoyed so much watching these Westerns with him. I guess it makes me feel close to him again in a funny way. I loved my dad.

Teacher, 52, white woman, Mississippi

It takes me back to the Fox theatre in St. Louis when my family would go to the movies every week and Westerns were plentiful. There was no graphic sex or violence. Movies were truly entertainment. My favorite Western (Rio Bravo) brings all of this back to me and gives me hope.

High school fine arts administrator, 49, white man

Always have loved Westerns. Western stars were the heroes of the '40s in pre-TV days. Dad always took us to town to see the Saturday night Westerns at the local movie house.

Retired geologist, 63, white woman, Wisconsin

When I was very young, my father used to take me and my siblings to the drive-in. We went almost every Friday night during the summer and invariably we watched Westerns. I think my father influenced my love of Westerns a great deal.

Program administrator, 49, white woman, Rhode Island

In some ways, growing up with Westerns is a quiet singularity, an individual experience that holds a special place for the adult who looks back. In other ways, it is a shared experience that saw millions of families relaxing, having fun together, and establishing a strong bond transcending both subtle and substantial differences across the generations. For fans looking back, these memories connect them with their past, connect them with their families, and take them away from the stresses of day-to-day life. As they describe the emotions they experience while watching their favorite Westerns, they talk about feeling secure, comforted, happy, content, and hopeful.

They are comforting and remind me of watching TV on weekends with my father.

Business development coordinator, 37, white woman, Missouri

They make me feel like I'm ten years old again. That warm safe feeling of watching different shows with my brothers and sisters at home when I was little. They just make me think of my childhood. It's kind of nice to remember a time when you didn't have to worry about anything and society wasn't so bad.

Legal secretary, 55, black woman, Rhode Island

Having been raised with TV Westerns, watching them induces secure feelings from childhood.

Elementary school librarian, 55, white woman, Kansas

Westerns give expression to innocence and appeal to fans' desire for simplicity and an escape from contemporary worries.

Reminds me of a time when there was less stress—an age of innocence, so to speak. Also reminds me greatly of growing up—watching these Westerns with my dad.

Laborer/teacher, 52, white man, Massachusetts

In short, watching their favorite Westerns makes fans feel good—and what more could a genre ask for?

CHAPTER 4

THE COWBOY WAY

"Fill your hands, you son of a bitch!"

John Wayne in *True Grit*

John Wayne as Marshal Rooster
Cogburn in *True Grit* (1969),
courtesy Photofest

With these words, John Wayne, as one-eyed Marshal
Rooster Cogburn, took his reins in his teeth and charged
across an aspen-enclosed meadow, firing double-fisted from
his rifle and pistol. When the smoke had cleared, his horse
was dead, but he had killed three of the four outlaws who were
arrogant enough to think they could take him on (the fourth
had turned and run).

This is the Western hero the way we love him. He may not
be perfect. He may swear, he may drink, he may be carrying a
bit too much around the middle, but he is defiant, skilled, courageous,
indomitable. He will never give in—not to the elements, not to adversity,
not to pain, not to any man or woman:

"Git!"

"Maybe I will—but likely I won't."

J. P. Lockney and Tom Mix, *Just Tony* (1922)

"Nobody asked you to come here."

"Well I'm here, and I'm going to stay here. This town better get used to the idea."

Donald Crisp and James Stewart, *The Man From Laramie* (1955)

"You want to quit Ethan?"

"That'll be the day."

Ward Bond and John Wayne, *The Searchers* (1956)

At his most romantic, the cinematic Man of the West leads a life of adventure and almost constant danger. He is willing to stand up for his principles and die in defense of his friends, family, and/or community. With a keen eye and cool head, he dispatches with pinpoint accuracy and deadly speed those who do him wrong or otherwise stand against him. We know what he will do in just about any situation—there is no accommodation, no compromise. He is dogged, determined, relentless:

"I'll kill the first man who so much as whispers a word about giving up."

Yul Brynner, *The Magnificent Seven* (1960)

"When things look bad and it looks like you're not going to make it, then you gotta get mean. I mean plumb, mad-dog mean. Cuz if you lose your head and you give up, then you neither live nor win."

Clint Eastwood, *The Outlaw Josey Wales* (1976)

"Tell all the other curs the law's comin'. Tell 'em I'm comin'. And Hell's comin' with me!"

Kurt Russell, *Tombstone* (1993)

The Western hero follows a "code"—loyalty to comrades, defense and protection of the weak, honor above all else. He has nothing personal at stake…except his integrity. He won't desert his fellows:

"We're going to stick together just like it used to be. When you side with a man, you stay with him. And if you can't do that, you're like some animal. You're finished. We're finished!"

William Holden, *The Wild Bunch* (1969)

He won't stand by and let people be bullied, abused, exploited, or hurt:

> "That ain't right. I don't like what's not right."
>
>> Danny Glover, *Silverado* (1985)

He won't run from a fight:

> "There are just some things a man can't run away from."
>
>> John Wayne, *Stagecoach* (1939)

In the end, he remains true to his principles, whether those principles are popular or not. He will never bend to fit the fashion. His word is his bond:

> "Mister, when I give my word, I keep it."
>
>> John Wayne, *Hondo* (1953)

> "Money can't be the reason you took the job."
>
> "Can you think of a better reason?"
>
> "We gave our word. You gave your word to me."
>
>> Lee Marvin and Burt Lancaster, *The Professionals* (1966)

The characters that were portrayed were men that you could look up to and be proud of anytime. Even the bad guys had certain codes. Take care of women and children, keep your word, and stand up for what you believe in, even though their choice of professions was not very ethical (sometimes they even became lawmen— I'm sure I have some of them in my family tree from E. Texas).

Financial planner, 62, Native American woman, Texas

Butch Cassidy and the Sundance Kid brings up the warm feeling of belonging. The obvious care between the two characters was inspiring. They depended on one another to make their way in a hostile world. They "mattered" to one another, which is the bottom line for most of us.

Newspaper general manager, 54, white man, Minnesota

The good guy always places the underdog ahead of himself and strives to protect the innocent and helpless or more vulnerable person.

Product engineer, 65, white man, Pennsylvania

I like characters who are protective of others. I like those who stay because of a sense of duty even when everything in them says RUN! I expect this of myself and find I look for it in my heroes.

"Mom of all trades," 55, white woman, Ohio

"Buck, honey, you just one man."

"But I gave my word."

Ruby Dee and Sidney Poitier, *Buck and the Preacher* (1971)

A man of action, the traditional Western hero uses violence, but only reluctantly, as a last resort; he will never reach for his guns first, he will never shoot an unarmed man, and he will never shoot anyone in the back. Though he doesn't look for a fight, he will not hesitate to defend himself— and he'll do it with unparalleled skill, precision, and moral justification.

"If I can make them give up without a fight, I will."

Randolph Scott, *Santa Fe* (1951)

"What was I supposed to do? Just stand there and let that little boy shoot me full of holes?"

Gregory Peck, *The Gunfighter* (1950)

"I hate rude behavior in a man. Won't tolerate it."

Tommy Lee Jones, *Lonesome Dove* (1989)

The Western hero is bold, single-minded, quick to action, ready for anything. Such qualities come at a price, though. He is isolated and rootless. He saves the community, but is never part of it. He perseveres and succeeds despite overwhelming odds and utter exhaustion, but he is a wanderer, a loner. He is in command, mentally and physically. He is respected (sometimes feared). Conversation comes to a halt when he enters a room. But he must do battle, suffer, sacrifice...and move on:

"The only land I'll settle down on will be under a tombstone."

William S. Hart, *Tumbleweeds* (1925)

"I can't rightly say any place is my home."

James Stewart, *The Man from Laramie* (1955)

Most Westerns portray real men who would stand up for a cause, family, friends, and their homeland. There is a great deal of violence, but it's not like a gangster movie or a movie about the hood. In a Western, the violence is accepted and legit.

Postal clerk, 47, black woman, West Virginia

Tommy Lee Jones as Woodrow Call, *Lonesome Dove* (1989), courtesy Photofest

Yul Brynner as Chris
Adams, *The Magnificent
Seven* (1960), courtesy
Photofest

*I grieve when the innocent
suffer and like to see them
vindicated, not so much vic-
tims avenged as evil overcome. Randolph Scott was my
favorite Western actor, always
a gentleman, and, like Gary
Cooper, a person of integrity.
Today, Clint Eastwood incor-
porates the ambiguities of our
time into such a character. I
am a congenial loner and I like
to see those characteristics on
the screen.*

> Retired secondary teacher/
> parish priest, 69, white
> man, Indiana

*The better Westerns have a
tendency towards romanti-
cized role models of fair-hand-
edness, judicial righteousness,
and independent spirituality.
The protagonists are largely
free spirits who believe in and
follow a rigorous moral code,
without feeling the contemporary necessity to bend this
code to fit the fashion. They
are tenacious heroes who are
not prone to surrender.*

> Retail salesman, 57, white
> man, Minnesota

"Places you are tied down to—none. People with a hold on you—
none."

> Yul Brynner, *The Magnificent Seven* (1960)

"Dyin' ain't so hard for men like you and me. It's livin' that's hard."

> Clint Eastwood, *The Outlaw Josey Wales* (1976)

Regardless of their backgrounds, Western fans enjoy the cinematic
Man of the West for his single-mindedness and resolve. Such terms as
"decisive," "independent," "strong," "macho," "enigmatic," "tenacious,"
"loyal," and "honorable" are used consistently throughout descriptions
that express admiration for the hero's "leadership," "self-sacrifice," "defense of the weak," "doing what he must despite overwhelming odds,"
and "keeping true to his word." Many who love Westerns look to their
heroes as role models, both for themselves and society at large.

*Everyone needs heroes. I learned that certain things are right and must
be defended. John Wayne rescuing the girl in* The Searchers, Shane

helping the homesteaders against the rich, cruel cattleman, the men who believed in freedom to the point of death in The Alamo, *Henry Fonda returning to his men to die with them in* Fort Apache, *and* The Magnificent Seven *restoring dignity to the Mexican villagers.*

> Insurance broker assistant vice president, 39, white woman, Texas

I feel that if I emulate the character of the portrayed Western hero, it empowers me and allows me to gain the respect of others.

> Associate medical director (physician executive), 65, white man, Rhode Island

Of course, enjoying the cinematic Man of the West is not simply a matter of admiring (or emulating) character traits. The real fun for Western fans is "being there," either in a visceral sense or being swept up by the action, particularly the final resolution when good uncompromisingly defeats evil.

I enjoy the sense of adventure in Rio Bravo. *If I had been in that place at that time, I would have helped defend the jail. In my very wild imagination, I am there—helping the Duke save the West!*

> Hospital purchasing manager, 45, white woman, Missouri

In addition, because most plots are simple, with good and evil clearly delineated, many enjoy Westerns because they find a couple of hours lost in the West of the silver screen a welcome respite from everyday stresses and the relative morality of the "real world." In fact, there is a comforting satisfaction in watching good defeat *unquestioning* evil.

In Westerns, the "good" characters are able to solve their problems in quick, simple ways—usually with a gun. By watching Westerns, one is able to kill EVIL over and over again, in a symbolic sense. In life, it is hard to determine what is always "bad" or evil; "good" and "bad" are usually found in mixtures. In reality, bullets kill "good" and "bad" together. It certainly makes one feel good to be able to rid the world of "bad," even if it has to be done in symbolic or vicarious ways.

> Secondary school teacher, 39, white man, North Carolina

Of course, some experience this satisfaction more keenly than others:

One lesson I learned was that you couldn't trust the bad guy to help out his friends if they were hurt and wounded in the final shootout. More often than not, he would put them out of their misery with a bullet or some such double-cross! This was more effective than a moralistic speech about hanging out with bad companions!

> Newspaper advertising sales rep, 60, white man, New Hampshire

I love Westerns for the hero, the embodiment of character values—courage, honor, honesty, importance of family, reluctance to use force to gain advantage, proper use of force in self-defense, attempting to impose order on a chaotic world.

> Market research interviewer, 52, white woman, Arkansas

Feelings of being there, i.e., when the rider is soaking wet and cold, you can feel it. When he must shoot his horse, you feel his sorrow. When surrounded by hostile Indians, you feel the same, "aaawwww s___!"

> Retired van/bus driver, 72, white man, Massachusetts

With Westerns, the plots are simple—good versus bad. It's easy to get emotional and pulled into them. Before long, I want to wear a hat, boots, and six-guns, and ride into one of those towns and shoot it out with the bad guys!

> Foreman, 60, white man, Virginia

From left to right, Rick Nelson and John Wayne, *Rio Bravo* (1959), courtesy Photofest

Things are black and white. Clearly easy to see right and wrong, no gray areas. The bank robbers, horse or cattle thieves, renegade Indians are always clearly the "bad guys." Not necessarily true in real life. Not complicated usually, easy to follow, unlike real life. A true "escape" from the day to day confusion daily living brings, a "no-brainer," as they say. Real entertainment.

Bank manager, 61, white woman, Colorado

Just always enjoyed a good shoot-'em-up. Sometimes I felt bad for the bad guy—it seemed to relate to me; at a certain time in my life I was a bad guy. But mostly when the good guy rode off into the sunset, I wished that I could be a good guy and everything would end happily.

Helicopter production manager, 63, black man, Pennsylvania

I kind of like the idea of pulling out my Colt and blowing away assholes who bug me (well, the fantasy, anyway).

Service area coordinator, 53, white woman, California

Ultimately, Western fans identify with the hero (and sometimes the villain). They admire the hero's traits and long to walk in his boots. After all, as this man notes:

Don't we all want to be the good guy who rides into town and saves the good townsfolk from the evil land baron?

Letter carrier, 50, white man, Arizona

Western heroes have had many faces over the years. For fans, the very term "Western hero" conjures up images of favored actors—Gene Autry, Roy Rogers, William Boyd, Randolph Scott, John Wayne, Gary Cooper,

James Stewart, Gregory Peck, Alan Ladd, Joel McCrea, Clint Eastwood. But two iconographic cinematic westerners are hands-down audience favorites, representing two very different types of heroes. Not surprisingly, they are: John Wayne and Clint Eastwood. Slightly more than half of Western fans choose a movie featuring one or the other as their favorite, with 37% choosing one starring the Duke and 19% choosing one with Clint Eastwood.

WESTERN STAR PREFERENCES

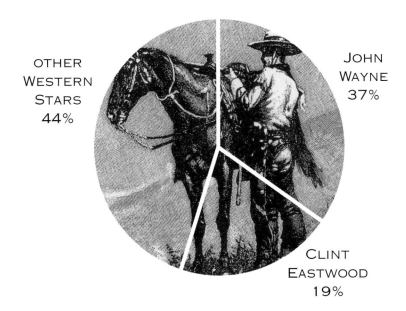

OTHER WESTERN STARS 44%

JOHN WAYNE 37%

CLINT EASTWOOD 19%

Based on interviews with 500 Western fans

Though it may at first seem from these numbers that John Wayne is the clear favorite, there is more here than meets the eye. First, John Wayne simply made more Westerns (40 to 50 Bs and about 35 big budgets, versus Clint Eastwood's ten big budgets), so there are more John Wayne Westerns to choose from. More interesting, though, are the demographic differences in audience preference. John Wayne *is* the clear favorite, but only among certain groups: women, older people (those age 45 and older), and whites. Men, younger people (under 45), and people of color enjoy John Wayne and Clint Eastwood fairly equally.

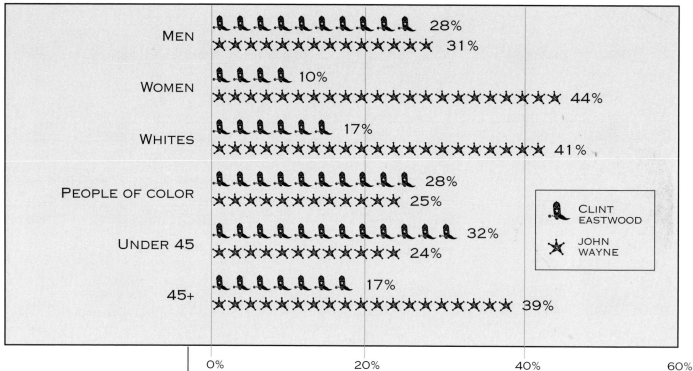

Based on interviews with 500 Western fans

None of this is really surprising. That women tend to prefer the warmth and humor of John Wayne's larger than life leader/mentor over the cold, hard edge of Clint Eastwood's mercenary/avenger makes sense. Wayne's more traditional hero is concerned about the community; he may stand apart from it, but he cares about it, respects it, protects it. When he kills, he does so reluctantly and for a greater good. Women are drawn to this type of hero. With Eastwood, however, there is no reluctance around violence; his characters are almost machinelike in their ability to assess a situation and act swiftly and lethally, something men would more likely tend to enjoy.

As for the racial differences, again, this makes some sense. John Wayne has a reputation, whether justified or not, for being racially intolerant. Certainly he made movies during a time of more flagrant racist attitudes. Also, many of his movies feature battles against Indians (the cavalry trilogy, *The Searchers*), and not necessarily showing Indians in the best light, which puts race front and center (often problematically). By contrast, there are very few Indians, or people of color at all, for that

*John Wayne's character is usu-
ally independent, fair, honest,
and respectful of women.*

> Credit/collections supervi-
> sor, white woman, Rhode
> Island

*I don't like violent Westerns,
like the Clint Eastwood ones.
I don't think they represent the
true West at all. There couldn't
have been that much killing for
almost no reason.*

> Homemaker, 71, white
> woman, Minnesota

matter, in Clint Eastwood's Westerns, so race really isn't a factor. This doesn't mean John Wayne isn't popular among people of color—quite the contrary! But it does mean his popularity isn't quite as high as it is among whites.

And in terms of the age difference, there is no question both actors have a generational appeal—Wayne represents the type of Westerner popular in the late 1940s and 1950s, whereas Eastwood's era is more the 1960s and 1970s. As one fan put it:

> I didn't live in the John Wayne era. If you want to know about John Wayne, that's a question for my parents.
>
> Construction company owner, 38, Latino man, Central America

People relate to those movies that either reflect something in their own lives or project some sort of fantasy of how they'd like their lives to be. Wayne is older in many of his Westerns, assuming leadership roles with social responsibility. Eastwood is younger, more of a free spirit, going where he pleases when he pleases.

The cinematic Man of the West has certainly changed a great deal over the past 100 years, as the heroic types embodied by these two men demonstrate. Westerns, after all, as with any popular cultural form, reflect their era. John Wayne himself noted he infused the hero with his own brand of common sense. As he told one interviewer:

> Following my dad's advice, if a guy hit me with a vase, I'd hit him with a chair. That's the way we played it. I changed the saintly Boy Scout of the original cowboy hero into a more normal kind of fella.

The 1910's and early 1920's realism of William S. Hart gave way to Tom Mix's fancy showmanship by the end of the silent era, a style that served as a precursor to the B Western stars of the 1930s and early 1940s. These Westerns embraced an unencumbered American spirit and vitality that celebrated fairness and democracy, a morally flawless image. The great westward march, with its rugged pioneers confronting the hardships of the savage wilderness and prevailing, was the perfect metaphor for a newly emergent international power. Such films as *The Covered Wagon* (1923), the first truly epic Western and one of the highest-grossing silent films, and *Tumbleweeds* (1925), William S. Hart's paean to the 1889 Cherokee Strip

Clint Eastwood as Hogan, *Two Mules for Sister Sara* (1970), courtesy Photofest

In The Shootist, *John Wayne gave us the rules to live by. All Westerns give us a piece of the truth, but in this movie it was pointed out to us, for all to know, and left no doubt that it was right.*

Salesman, 53, Latino man, Colorado

Westerns are an interesting mirror for the times during which the Western was made. (Westerns of the '20s offered a far simpler, more clear-cut distinction between "good" and "bad" than a Western of the '90s like Clint Eastwood's Unforgiven.)

Retail banker, 54, black woman, Kansas

land rush in Oklahoma (which opened three million acres of Indian land to white settlers and speculators), glorified the frontier past as an unqualified righteous history. And though few big-budget Westerns were made during the Depression and World War II, the B Westerns, with their singing cowboys and easily identified heroes and villains, continued to give voice to American innocence.

In the early 1940s, fueled by the success of John Ford's *Stagecoach* (1939) and a spate of outlaw-turned-hero movies (e.g., *Jesse James, Return of Frank James, When the Daltons Rode*), studios began again to invest in big-budget Westerns. And it was during this period the Western hero underwent a significant transition, with several films that bore the hallmarks of the matured "adult," "social," or "psychological" Western

Jane Russell as Rio, *The Outlaw* (1943), courtesy Photofest

The Ox-Bow Incident *reinforces my strong belief that laws are basic to the strength and survival of civilization. Without law that is evenhandedly imposed, chaos, greed, and unfettered self-interest would rule, breaking down the very fabric of humankind and civilization. The Ox Bow Incident makes the point very clearly and persuasively.*

Attorney, 46, white man, Pennsylvania

so successful in the 1950s. Howard Hughes's *The Outlaw* (1943), for example, is credited with introducing sex into the Western. A far more powerful movie, however, is *The Ox-Bow Incident*, released that same year. William Wellman's bleak film has no hero per se, but tells the story of three cowboys who are hanged on very flimsy evidence for stealing cattle, a crime they did not commit. Westerners in this film are cast under a pall of malice and suspicion, a thoroughgoing reversal of frontier morality that would not reappear in the Western until the 1960s. But it did introduce a psychological dimension that would become popular by the end of the decade.

The Western as it emerged in the 1950s was rooted in two concurrent trends. On the one hand, the epic scope and traditional heroism of such films as *Wagon Master* (1950), *The Big Country* (1958), and *The Alamo* (1960) reflected a triumphant post-World War II America facing down the evils of Communism and global instability. America emerged from World War II a military, industrial, and technological power, particularly as compared to the nearly decimated countries of the European and Asian continents—a sign, many felt, of American superiority and invincibility, proof that America's position as leader of the free world was well deserved and justifiable. This conviction, grounded in a long tradition of viewing America as a republic with a divine mission, was only reinforced when the full extent of the murderous horrors perpetrated by the Axis nations

Three cowboys are about to be wrongly hanged in *The Ox-Bow Incident* (1943), courtesy Photofest

Right: Gregory Peck as James McKay in *The Big Country* (1958), courtesy Photofest

Below: John Wayne as Davy Crockett in *The Alamo* (1960), courtesy Photofest

was revealed. The mass slaughter of innocent civilians and the brutality toward American prisoners of war stood in marked contrast to vaunted ideals of equality, democracy, freedom of religion, and freedom of speech, further widening a perceived gap separating American "civilization" from world "savagery." In this context, Westerns celebrated a great heritage and unlimited capabilities. That the hero's strength and power were exerted only in the face of severe provocation, exercised with the utmost restraint, and only against unqualified evil, reflected America's vision of itself in the international arena.

On the other hand, the brooding, isolated hero of such films as *High Noon* (1952), *Shane* (1953), and *The Searchers* (1956) was a product of

an undercurrent of malaise. The flush of total victory in World War II, followed by the unprecedented prosperity of the 1950s, gave cinematic Westerners their heroic quality. But McCarthyism, the Cold War, and concerns about growing suburbanization and the loss of individuality and independence, particularly in corporate America, gave Western heroes a tragic edge. No longer the fresh-faced kids of a 1930s Gene Autry or Roy Rogers, Western heroes in the 1950s were older, many with weathered faces and haunted eyes. John Wayne as Ethan Edwards in *The Searchers* (1956) looks out at us half-smiling, but his unshaven face and the lines around his eyes and those that crease his forehead suggest a life that has seen more of hardship and death than any man should.

In fact, of all Western stars, John Wayne is the quintessential embodiment of this type of more complex 1950s hero, and arguably one of the most convincing actors ever to don spurs. It would be difficult to

John Wayne as Ethan Edwards in *The Searchers* (1956), courtesy Photofest

find a star to match his stature and longevity; more than two decades after his death in 1979, he still ranks as one of America's *all-time favorite* movie stars. No wonder so many Western fans, even today, choose him as their number one cowboy.

Already 32 years old when he began his rise to stardom, with the leading role in John Ford's classic *Stagecoach* (1939), John Wayne gradually perfected an on-screen image of the rugged individualist and man of action, becoming, eventually, an American patriarch. Significantly, most of his movies feature an intergenerational plot whereby Wayne's character teaches soldiers or cowboys how to behave forthrightly and courageously through a series of initiations, ranging from fistfights to gunfights to warfare. Through his heroes—older battle-tested sergeants, former Civil War officers (Union and Confederate), gunfighters, marshals, and cowmen—Wayne continues to teach generations of audiences what it means to be an American, what it means to be a man.

> *In my opinion, there has been no better teacher of how to be a man by example than Duke Wayne. My favorite Westerns all have Duke Wayne in them. When the Duke was on the screen, he made me believe he was not acting, that that was his true persona up there. The characters the Duke portrayed mostly all had strong convictions of what was right or wrong. Duke Wayne was believable. He was a man's man, a role model for me when I was growing up.*
>
> Banker, 44, white man, Illinois

John Wayne, as a screen persona and as an individual, successfully articulated and transmitted an enormously popular and highly resonant ideal, one which embodied personal power, courage, honor, and just plain common sense.

> "Never apologize, Mister. It's a sign of weakness."
>
> as Captain Nathan Brittles, *She Wore a Yellow Ribbon* (1949)

> "I mean to kill you in one minute, Ned, or see you hanged in Fort Smith at Judge Parker's convenience. Which'll it be?"
>
> as Marshal Rooster Cogburn, *True Grit* (1969)

> "I won't be wronged, I won't be insulted, and I won't be laid a hand on. I don't do these things to other people and I require the same from them."
>
> as J. B. Books, *The Shootist* (1976)

Wayne was fond of recalling what he considered his father's best advice: Keep your word, never intentionally insult anyone, and don't look for trouble—but if trouble finds you, make sure you win. In everything he did, he endeavored to stay true to these precepts.

Off-screen, Wayne made no secret of his right-wing beliefs, including a lifelong conviction that the spread of Communism presented the most serious threat not only to American security but to the future of democracy around the world. Despite studio warnings that his affiliation

John Wayne as Ringo Kid in *Stagecoach* (1939), courtesy Photofest

John Wayne meant so much to me as I grew up; he is the main reason I love Westerns. My own father taught me very little. All he was interested in was a good time with booze and women. I looked to John Wayne for inspiration and to know how a real man should be. In all his movies, he never let me down, and no one could convince me that the real Duke was not the one I saw on the screen.

Construction manager and design consultant, 60, white man, Ohio

John Wayne is not violent unless provoked or others are in danger. What you see is what you get. No airs—just down-to-earth and a genuine hero.

Homemaker, 66, white woman, California

John Wayne with his young charges in *The Cowboys* (1972), courtesy Photofest

with the Motion Picture Alliance for the Preservation of American Ideals, an anti-communist organization, would ruin his career, Wayne served as president from 1949 to 1952, all the while enjoying enormous popularity.

From left to right, John Wayne and Montgomery Clift, *Red River* (1948), courtesy Photofest

Ultimately, John Wayne's name became synonymous with an entire cultural ideal, one so powerfully resonant that the mere mention of his name even today elicits the notions of strength, courage, and patriotism. Fans love him for his determination, no-nonsense attitude, and sheer tenacity. Even if they don't agree with his political views, they admire what he stands for. Says one fan:

> *I don't prescribe to all of John Wayne's political or social views, but I admire his ability to stick by them despite all the consequences. Most times when I see John Wayne movies, I envision him as a father figure, the type of father I would have liked to have had. He also reminds me of the type of person I would like to be, especially in later life.*
>
> Researcher, 48, white man, New York

John Wayne continued to make very popular (and profitable) Westerns in the 1960s and into the '70s, winning his only Academy Award in 1970 for his performance as Rooster Cogburn in *True Grit* (1969). His final performance as the fatally ill J. B. Books in *The Shootist* (1976) was a poignant ending to his career, paralleling his own battle with cancer and death just three years later.

Wayne played a similar type of character throughout these years, but, concurrently, other filmmakers began using Westerns as a way to voice a more pronounced frustration and anger. The 1950s were hardly halcyon days, but it wasn't until the mid to late 1960s that many Americans felt confronted by a looming gulf between precious ideals and cold reality. Great expectations, inflated by an unquestioning belief in American moral superiority and unlimited capabilities, fueled by victory in World War II and unprecedented postwar economic expansion, were being shattered by the realities of Vietnam, antiwar unrest at home, an unfulfilled civil rights agenda, and, eventually, stagflation (inflation and recession) and Watergate. By the mid-1970s, a broad spectrum of Americans found themselves challenging deeply held beliefs and assumptions that were at one time thought unassailable: America, the defender of freedom around the world; America, the haven against persecution; America, the land of unlimited opportunity.

From the mid-1960s through the early 1970s, this more disillusioned America produced a different sort of Western hero, one far more jaded and cynical, an antihero battling an increasingly corrupt society in which the line between good and evil was ambiguous and blurred.

"It's the good guys against the bad guys. Question is—who are the good guys?"

Burt Lancaster, *The Professionals* (1966)

Films like *The Professionals* (1966), *Butch Cassidy and the Sundance Kid* (1969), and, most notably, *The Wild Bunch* (1969) featured antiheroes (generally outlaws with no intention of "going straight") who had little in common with their traditional predecessors. With the exception of personal integrity and lethal skills, these antiheroes showed no inclination

Once Upon a Time in the West *takes on all the myths of the West. Some of the myths end up trashed, some seem ridiculed. The whole film seems as earthy as the West actually was. I mean, Henry Fonda is a child killer. The heroine uses sex appeal to guarantee her protection. No one here is too clean.*

Retail salesman, 40, white man, South Carolina

to sacrifice themselves for a larger community. But why should they? The frontier in these Westerns was arid and lifeless, populated by sycophants and hypocrites whose most pronounced character traits were greed and pettiness. Defense of this type of community would seem at the very least oddly misplaced.

Just as John Wayne embodied the complex, sober hero of the 1950s, so Clint Eastwood came to represent this antiestablishment, antiauthority hero of the 1960s and 1970s. Long and lanky, a man of few words but deadly action, Eastwood's heroes are aloof, detached, emotionless. His laconic manner, jingling spurs, and signature squint—half suspicion, half irritation at being bothered—give his characters an aura of tension and danger.

Clint Eastwood's first major role had little in common with the mysterious stranger he would make famous. As Rowdy Yates in television's *Rawhide*, which began its seven year run in 1959, Eastwood played an easygoing cowboy, very much within the parameters of the traditional type so popular at that time. But the role wasn't terribly interesting for Eastwood and when an opportunity arose to play outside type during *Rawhide*'s 1964 hiatus, Eastwood took it. As he told an interviewer in 1997:

> You know, your average Western, the hero's got to step forth and grab the guy who's shooting the kid or something like that. But this guy doesn't do anything; he turns and rides away. And I thought, "That is perfect. That's something I've always wanted to do in a Western."

Italian director Sergio Leone offered Eastwood the chance to star in *A Fistful of Dollars*, a remake of Akira Kurosawa's classic *Yojimbo*. The part had been offered to both Charles Bronson and James Coburn, but they had turned it down. With a free trip to Europe and $15,000 for his efforts, Eastwood figured if the film flopped, no one would see it anyway. Little did he know he would end up making a total of three films for Leone, and, in the process, redefine the Western hero.

Where the traditional Man of the West disdains the notion of selling his gunfighting expertise (the gun for hire is generally the villain in traditional Westerns), Eastwood's "No Name" mercenary (he does actually have a name in these movies—United Artists billed him as "The Man

Opposite: From left to right, Paul Newman and Robert Redford, *Butch Cassidy and the Sundance Kid* (1969), courtesy Photofest

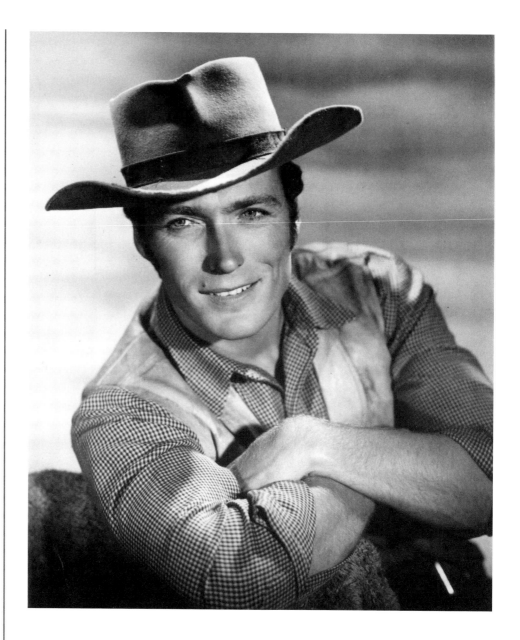

With No Name" as a marketing ploy when *A Fistful of Dollars* was released
in the United States in 1967) unashamedly counts the cash he makes by
selling his services to both sides in *A Fistful of Dollars*. He matter-of-factly
adds up the thousands coming to him when the body count is complete
in *For a Few Dollars More,* and in *The Good, the Bad and the Ugly,* he
vies with two other mercenaries to find a horde of Confederate gold.

> "Baxters over there. Rojos there. Me right in the middle. There's
> money to be made in a place like this."
>
> as Joe in *A Fistful of Dollars* (1964)

"16 thousand dollars...17...22...22? [gun blasts] 27."

as Monco in *For a Few Dollars More* (1965)

"If I get killed you'll never get your hands on all that beautiful money."

as Blondie in *The Good, the Bad and the Ugly* (1966)

Eastwood left the gun for hire behind in most of his subsequent Westerns, but he continued to play the mysterious stranger, a man of few words, devoid of emotion or sympathy, disconnected from a broader social community. Even his heroes who did come to the defense of others did so reluctantly.

"I suppose that mangy red-boned hound ain't got no place else to go either. He might as well ride along with us. Hell, everybody else is."

as Josey Wales in *The Outlaw Josey Wales* (1976)

While many John Wayne fans feel the Duke stands as a model of manhood and social responsibility, Eastwood fans are drawn to his

Bad guys are ugly, dirty, very mean. In For a Few Dollars More, *Clint demonstrates that the good guy once again has better strategy as well as gunfighting skills. This is a very mean and violent movie, but good triumphs without being goody-goody. The cinematography presents things so real you can almost smell the dirt and sweat.*

Postal window clerk, 56, white man, Illinois

Clint Eastwood as Joe in *A Fistful of Dollars* (1964), courtesy Photofest

The violence, the action is what I like about Clint Eastwood. He's a rough guy, not a role model. I wouldn't call him a bad guy. It's just a movie. The guy was mayor of Carmel, California, right? So he can't be all that bad. It's just an image he portrays—very macho type of actor, very rough, "make my day."

Construction company owner, 38, Latino man, Central America

He's cool. He is just cool!

Sales manager, 46, white man, New York

Clint Eastwood as Josey Wales in *The Outlaw Josey Wales* (1976), courtesy Photofest

characters' reserve and low-key demeanor. They don't talk about him as a role model; they emphasize action and excitement and describe Eastwood as rough and macho. They are drawn to the visceral grittiness of his movies, their hard, cold edge. They also find him cool, in control of every situation. As this fan states,

> *I like the way Clint Eastwood acts—how calm he is. He always thinks things through. Nothing bothers or phases him.*
>
> Outdoors receiver at a home center, 26, white man

Few Westerns have been made in the last 20 years, but this is hardly the end of the story. Not only do filmmakers continue to craft tales of the Old West, though infrequently—Kevin Costner's *Open Range* and Ron Howard's *The Missing* (both in 2003) are the most recent examples—but

Kevin Costner as Charley
Waite in *Open Range* (2003),
courtesy Photofest

Western heroes continue to ride tall in the popular imagination, delighting fans both old and new. Heroes may be grittier (and dirtier) than their 1930s predecessors, their language may be more "colorful" (HBO's series *Deadwood* gives new definition to the term), and they may be quicker to draw their guns, but their courage, perseverance, and steely-eyed determination remain unchanged. For many fans, stories of adventure featuring strong-willed and tenacious heroes (no matter when they were made) are as meaningful today as they ever were.

Clint Eastwood as Blondie in *The Good, the Bad and the Ugly* (1966), courtesy Photofest

CHAPTER 5

THE TOP TEN FAVORITE WESTERNS

Clint Eastwood as William Munny in *Unforgiven* (1992), courtesy Photofest

Fans have many favorite Westerns. In fact, of the 1,052 fans interviewed for this book, over 100 *different* Westerns were named as favorites, from *Gunfight at the O.K. Corral* (1957) to *Blazing Saddles* (1974), *Westward the Women* (1951) to *Will Penny* (1968), *The Ox-Bow Incident* (1943) to *Young Guns* (1988)—most by just one or two people. But there are some movies that are more popular than others.

The top ten favorite movie Westerns according to this survey are listed on the following two pages. See what you think!

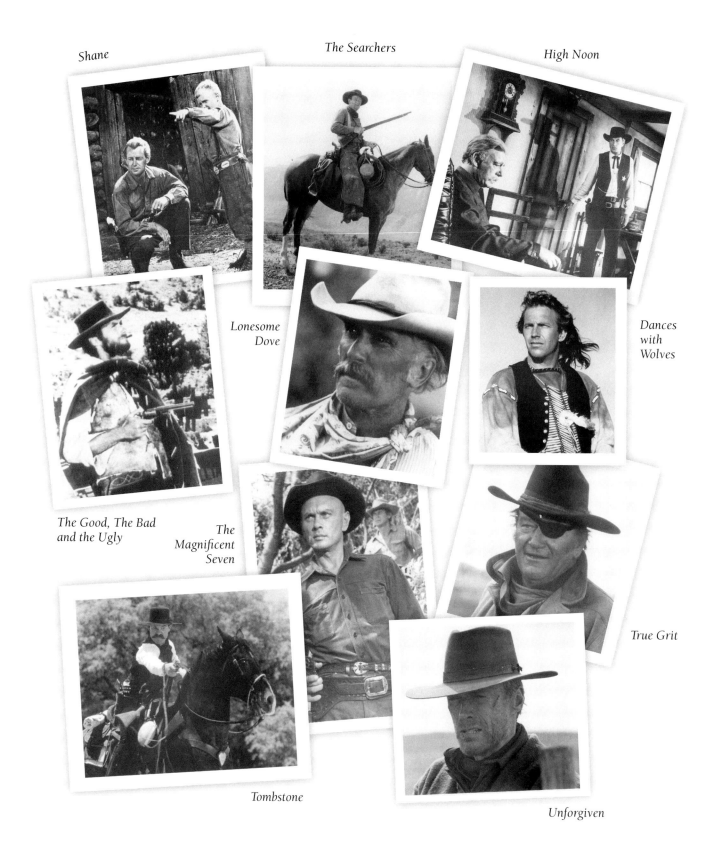

Shane

The Searchers

High Noon

Lonesome
Dove

Dances
with
Wolves

The Good, The Bad
and the Ugly

The
Magnificent
Seven

True Grit

Tombstone

Unforgiven

THE TOP TEN FAVORITE WESTERNS

The Top 10 Favorite Westerns

1. SHANE (1953)

2. THE SEARCHERS (1956)

3. HIGH NOON (1952)

4. THE GOOD, THE BAD AND THE UGLY (1966)

5. LONESOME DOVE (TV MINISERIES, 1989)

6/7. DANCES WITH WOLVES (1990) AND TRUE GRIT (1969) [TIED]

8. TOMBSTONE (1993)

9. THE MAGNIFICENT SEVEN (1960)

10. UNFORGIVEN (1992)

Lists of "top" movies (or "top" anything, for that matter) are by nature problematic—we want to see them, but we rarely agree with them. Such may be the case for you here. But, taken as a whole, the movies on this top ten list represent everything fans love about Westerns: an "authentic" Old West experience, riveting action, gripping human drama, indomitable heroes, nostalgia for a time gone by, magnificent landscapes. As we have seen, the primary reason people love Westerns is realism, and these favorites give many fans a sense of "being there." Through both a perceived historical accuracy and an emotional connection—stories, costumes, and geographies transporting viewers into the Old West with characters facing dilemmas, making decisions, and taking actions that resonate with them on a personal level—these movies satisfy longings to know what it was "really" like to live on the frontier. They enable fans to explore the human condition or simply fantasize about an imagined life of adventure with no ties and no modern responsibilities, especially with those shootouts, chase scenes, stampedes, fistfights, blizzards, and dust storms thrown in!

Through it all, of course, the individuals portrayed must have believable experiences, wrestle with believable conflict, and make believable decisions. This last piece is pivotal: Yes, historic accuracy is important, but the *realism* comes when viewers relate to and identify with the characters, particularly heroes, on a personal level. Do the representations ring true? How realistic are the decisions characters face, their dilemmas, struggles? After all, if the characters and their actions are not believable, how else can we experience what it might have been like to live on the frontier? Honest emotion, sacrifice, something to admire, aspire to, root for—characters with these attributes energize and entertain fans.

The Westerns on the top ten favorites list share these characteristics, capturing the frontier spirit: the strength, honor, courage, determination, and perseverance fans believe were required to survive and prevail in a hostile, often unyielding environment. The movies themselves, however, are quite different from one another. A combination of classic and more recent Westerns, they reflect a vast array of tastes and preferences. Some tend to appeal more to men than to women, to whites than to people of color, to older than to younger viewers—and vice versa. Some appeal to modern sensibilities, whereas others are long-time standards. Some tell rather conventional stories, but tell them extremely well, whereas others challenge audiences to think about the Western in new and different ways or use the genre to make pointed social commentary. Some offer disturbing representations of social relationships and historic events or bittersweet tales that fill audiences with a longing for a time gone by, whereas others offer rip-snortin' entertainment. All were hits in their day and continue to be strong audience draws.

#10 UNFORGIVEN (1992)

Producer/director Clint Eastwood presents a complex film in number ten on the favorite Westerns list. Unsentimental and hard-edged, *Unforgiven* tackles a familiar theme—an aging gunfighter who, despite trying to hang up his guns, cannot escape who he really is. But beyond this broad categorization, little about this film is traditional or familiar. William Munny may in many ways be Clint Eastwood's typically enig-

From let to right, Gene Hackman and Clint Eastwood in *Unforgiven* (1992), courtesy Photofest

Morgan Freeman as Ned Logan in *Unforgiven* (1992), courtesy Photofest

matic, laconic hero, but there is nothing heroic in what he does, except perhaps avenge his friend at the end of the film. Up to his elbows in mud, literally, as the film opens, he goes on one last job to bring home enough money to save his floundering hog farm and support his two children. Teaming up with his former partner (Morgan Freeman as Ned Logan) and a young gunman who calls himself the Schofield Kid (Jaimz Woolvett), he leads the effort to kill two cowboys who mutilated a prostitute and earn the bounty offered by her coworkers.

Tormented by regret over his past deeds, Munny wrestles with his decision. In feverish moments, he anguishes over his terrible guilt, both for killing again and for breaking the promise he made to his dead wife to abandon his former ways. With chilling brutality, *Unforgiven* presents a disquieting hero, a cold-blooded killer who has not been above murdering women and children in his marauding past and, despite heartfelt regrets, is still never far from the murderer in his soul. At the end of the film, after killing, among others, corrupt Sheriff Little Bill Daggett (Gene Hackman in an Oscar-winning role), Munny leaves the scene of the final shootout with the following admonition:

> "All right, I'm coming out. Any man I see out there I'm gonna kill him. Any son of a bitch takes a shot at me, I'm not only going to kill him, I'm going to kill his wife and all his friends and burn his damn house down. Nobody better shoot."

No one doubts he will make good on his threat.

Fans of this movie are drawn to what is, for them, an authentic presentation of the Old West, particularly in the character of William Munny. Many appreciate the shades of gray, an honest look at the essence of what Westerns have been glorifying for over 100 years—the killing, the lawlessness, romanticized murder. The Old West portrayed in this film is believable for these fans: an inhospitable, unforgiving environment where a brutal, ruthless gunman recognizes the evil in his past and tries to take a different path in life, but is compelled to return to what he knows in order to survive.

It was real, the feelings he had when he was killing people.

Owner of a management consulting firm, 58

Unforgiven was the movie that really got me interested in Westerns (I guess I came out of the "Western closet" with it, you could say). What I love about it is the way it takes Western myths and myth-makers and puts a human light on them. Unforgiven shows the Western is not all "guns and glory." It is a very dark, very gritty film exposing other Western myths. When watching Unforgiven, I feel like the Western is about people, not heroes. Then when I watch a Western about heroes, I can appreciate the need to create them (heroes) because, for the most part, they didn't exist.

30, Asian man, California

I like the way the characters in Unforgiven were developed. You see what happens to Clint Eastwood's character's mind. He regrets his occupation by movie's end even though he kills the "bad" man (Gene Hackman's sheriff).

Auto club dispatcher, 48, white woman, California

I like the fact that his character was gray—the lines of distinction between good and bad were blurred. Clint Eastwood was a murderer, but he had a heart.

Exotic dancer, 28, black man, Indiana

Despite the darker side of this Western, however, Clint Eastwood is controlled, cool, and deadly—just the way fans love him. In the final shootout, he easily guns down multiple opponents in riveting, fast action sequences. He may shoot the young cowboy who, having taken a bullet in the gut, lingers pitifully begging for water, but he also kills the sheriff we have come to despise in justifiable retaliation for the torture and murder of his long-time friend. Taken together, the action, emotion, and complex characterization that earned this Western Academy Awards for best picture, director, supporting actor, and editing also earn it a place as a top fan favorite.

#9 THE MAGNIFICENT SEVEN (1960)

Number nine on the top favorites list offers fans heroes who epitomize the frontier spirit. *The Magnificent Seven*, a remake of Akira Kurosawa's *Seven Samurai*, opens with a ruthless bandit terrorizing and looting a small Mexican town. The villagers, facing the choice of either abandoning their homes or fighting, send three representatives to a border town

From left to right, Yul Brynner, Steve McQueen, Horst Buchholz, Charles Bronson, Robert Vaughn, Brad Dexter, James Coburn in *The Magnificent Seven* (1960), courtesy Photofest

From left to right, Yul Brynner, Charles Bronson, and Brad Dexter teaching villagers how to shoot, *The Magnificent Seven* (1960), courtesy Photofest

to buy firearms. Guns being expensive, however, they hire gun*men* instead. Seven outcasts, led by Yul Brynner's Chris Adams, accompany the villagers back to their homes and lead a defense against the marauders.

Signing on for a mere $20, the Seven are lured by the opportunity to practice their dying craft and the exhilaration of a gunfight; they are not necessarily out to do a good deed. When Steve McQueen's character Vin scoffs at the low pay, one of the villagers tells him, "We understand. You could get much more in a grocery store. And it's good, steady work." McQueen's deadpan expression says it all. The life of stability and routine isn't for them; they're hired guns looking for their next job, and this is the only game in town.

As the movie progresses, however, the Seven develop an emotional bond with the villagers. They come to respect and even admire them, as Charles Bronson's character Bernardo O'Reilly makes clear to village children who say they are ashamed of their fathers:

> "You think I am brave because I carry a gun; well, your fathers are much braver because they carry responsibility, for you, your brothers, your sisters, and your mothers. And this responsibility is like a big rock that weighs a ton. It bends and it twists them

until finally it buries them under the ground. I have never had this kind of courage. Running a farm, working like a mule every day with no guarantee anything will ever come of it. This is bravery."

The Seven are significantly outnumbered and know the odds are against them, but they stay nonetheless. Yes, as traditional heroes, they have a strong sense of personal integrity and honor keeping them there. They stand by their word:

"You forget one thing. We took a contract."

"It's sure not the kind any court would enforce."

"That's just the kind you've got to keep."

    Yul Brynner and Steve McQueen

When captured but given the chance to leave so long as they don't return, they refuse. "Nobody throws me my own guns and says run," growls James Coburn as Britt, "nobody." But the idea of helping those who can't defend themselves is central to the film; in the end, the Seven cannot abandon the villagers who need them so desperately. And it is this notion of sacrifice that is especially appealing to many Western fans:

> The Magnificent Seven *is my favorite because seven lowlifes quit thinking of themselves. They think about others, they help others. They use their courage to make a town a safe place to live. They are willing to give up their lives for somebody else. Love the other person to make such a supreme sacrifice. They have no regrets while being outnumbered. Happy ending, the town is now safe for the farmers to live in.*
>
>   Baker, 50, white man, Oregon

> I love The Magnificent Seven *for the music, scenery, great actors (some at the start of long careers), the story of these gunfighters al-truistically going to help the Mexican villagers help themselves, won-derful dialogue, a fascinating villain, the tug-of-war between giving up and returning for the final fight, the little scenes of village life.*
>
>   Computer consultant, 60, white woman, Minnesota

Fans are drawn to the gamut of emotions expressed. There is strength: the Seven won't be intimidated, they won't be forced to abandon their

Steve McQueen as Vin in *The Magnificent Seven* (1960), courtesy Photofest

The Magnificent Seven *represents the perfect blend of actors, story, locale, and music. I get a charge just listening to the great Elmer Bernstein score. It instills in me an excitement unmatched by other films. What's more, the movie is always fresh to me. I never tire of seeing it over and over. Since the first time I saw it, it has provided me with enjoyment and thrills, the love of a good story, excellent team of actors, a rousing score, a suspenseful and riproaring screenplay, excellent cinematography, and superior direction by John Sturges.*

Retail clerk, 59, white man, Florida

responsibilities, they will win in the end (even at the cost of their own lives). But there is also sentiment: they bond with the villagers, feel sorrow and regret as they confront the loneliness in their lives, and place a higher priority on the villagers' safety than their own. Engrossing action sequences, seven charismatic actors (including Steve McQueen, Charles Bronson, James Coburn, and Robert Vaughn early in their careers), and one of the most memorable musical scores of any Western make *The Magnificent Seven* tops for many movie Western fans.

#8 TOMBSTONE (1993)

Number eight, *Tombstone*, has just about everything—perceived authenticity, gripping plot development and action, top-notch cinematography, and believable characters, particularly as presented in the relationship between Wyatt Earp (Kurt Russell) and Doc Holliday (Val Kilmer). *Tombstone* retells the familiar story of the gunfight at the O.K. Corral where retired Marshal Wyatt Earp and his brothers, along with Doc Holliday, faced members of the Clanton gang in a ferocious showdown. In this adaptation, though, the focus is more on the range war the gunfight ignited and Wyatt's obsessive mission to avenge the death of his younger brother by wiping out the larger outlaw group, The Cowboys. As a version for 1990s audiences, *Tombstone* offers characters that today's fans find believable and realistic: heroes who fear and loathe their darker sides ("already got a guilty conscience, might as well have the money, too," Wyatt Earp comments), but aren't afraid to emote or show their affection for one another; charismatic and vicious outlaws; and independent women.

For those who love this movie, the heroes in *Tombstone*, as others in the Westerns on the top ten list, epitomize the frontier spirit: strength

Wyatt Earp's fight is righteous—bad guys mess with the good guy, good guy beats bad guy. I also like that Doc Holliday, who's bordering on a scoundrel, is Wyatt's friend. Wyatt Earp is more of a conformist, follows the rules, is on the side of the law, where Doc Holliday is in the gray area. It's an unlikely friendship. I was never a fan of any Western until the Young Guns *movies and* Tombstone. *They move along faster.*

Truck driver/moving specialist, 31, white man, Massachusetts

From left to right, Val Kilmer, Sam Elliott, Kurt Russell, Bill Paxton, *Tombstone* (1993), courtesy Photofest

and courage to take risks and build a new life, dogged persistence to track down murderers and thieves who have terrorized family and community, loyalty and dedication to friends and comrades. In typical heroic fashion, Wyatt Earp is reluctant to act; he is a retired marshal come to Tombstone with his brothers to seek his fortune and establish a stable family life. Drawn into the fray when his brothers become lawmen, however, Earp turns deadly avenger when the killing spree culminates in the death of his younger brother. Wyatt, with friend Doc Holliday, hunts down members of the vicious Cowboy gang in ruthless fashion.

In addition to captivating heroes, *Tombstone* ranks highly among fans for its fierce action, emotionally charged and justifiable anger, but also downright fun. There is gripping drama (loss of friends and family) and riveting gunplay, but there are also fierce thunderstorms, relentless pursuits, clever dialogue, and humor. Evil gunman Johnny Ringo (Michael Biehn) and Doc Holliday, for example, exchange a demonstration of dexterity early on. Ringo displays his facility with firearms by twirling his pistol to the admiring saloon crowd. Doc responds by twirling a

I liked several of the characters in Tombstone, *particularly Doc Holliday. I liked the positive friendship presented between the main characters and the loyalty they have for each other. The happy ending was very satisfying. I liked Wyatt's love interest because she was so independent.*

Utility rate analyst, 53, white woman, Alabama

Tombstone *has a lot of real history and actual feelings of the people portrayed. As human beings, we all have a definite sense of right and wrong—this movie certainly crosses both boundaries back and forth— just like in real life.*

Business office manager, 54, white woman, Texas

From left to right, Val Kilmer and Kurt Russell in *Tombstone* (1993), courtesy Photofest

Val Kilmer as Doc Holliday in *Tombstone* (1993), courtesy Photofest

I just like Westerns, the actors. They are more handsome and real looking. I like the scenery, like Montana, or out West anywhere. I liked Val Kilmer in Tombstone. I liked him because he was handsome. I liked how he said, "I'm your huckleberry." There was a lot of action.

Bartender, 39, Native American woman, Massachusetts

I think a Stetson hat and a leather vest just makes a man look more handsome and rugged.

Retired bookkeeper, 75, white woman, Mississippi

When I drive to Oklahoma City from Amarillo on the interstate, I find myself looking out the window to the north. I always say that if I ever see anyone riding horseback across those hills, I am going to stop and wait for him.

Financial planner, 62, Native American woman, Texas

collapsible tin cup to the amusement of all. Last minute getaways, stunning landscapes and sunsets, fabulous horsemanship, despicable villains, first-rate costumes (flowing capes, cowboy duster coats), handlebar mustaches, pinpoint stares, and handsome leading men make the film a delight for fans to watch. In fact, many female fans echo the desire Dana

Delaney's character Josephine expresses when she lays eyes on Wyatt Earp for the first time:

"I wonder who that tall drink of water is?"

"My dear you have set your gaze upon the quintessential frontier type. Note the lean silhouette, eyes closed by the sun, they're sharp as a hawk. He's got the look of both predator and prey."

"I want one."

> Dana Delaney and Billy Zane

The last of their enemies killed or driven off, Doc Holliday succumbs to tuberculosis, but Wyatt Earp embraces a life of freedom and adventure with the high-spirited woman he loves. On his deathbed, Doc Holliday speaks for many fans when he pleads:

"Live every second, live right on through the end. Live Wyatt, live for me."

The combination of realistic settings and costumes, heart-stopping gunplay, vivid characterizations, and righteous vengeance creates a romanticized vision of freedom and adventure in the Old West that assures fans will continue to love this Western for years to come.

#6/7 TRUE GRIT (1969)

Tied with *Dances with Wolves* for number six on the favorite Westerns list, *True Grit* is a boisterous tribute to an aging and beloved Western star. A headstrong young girl looking for her father's killer hires an abrasive, hard-drinking marshal to track the man down and bring him in. Refusing to be left behind while the marshal (with a Texas Ranger) rides off on the killer's trail, she earns his respect as she follows and then joins the pursuit. A mixture of exuberance and sentimentality, excitement and warmth, *True Grit* measures up to its spectacular mountain landscapes by filling the screen with larger-than-life adventurers who possess the dogged determination and "grit" necessary to survive and prevail.

Tombstone is my favorite for the attention to costumes and language, for its authenticity. It explores such a romantic time period and a wide-open era. They could do anything and usually did. It's freedom at its essence!

> Self-employed, 31, white man, North Carolina

John Wayne as Marshal Rooster Cogburn, *True Grit* (1969), courtesy Photofest

From left to right, John Wayne and Kim Darby, *True Grit* (1969), courtesy Photofest

They showed John Wayne's character in True Grit *as an aged cowboy. He did not try to compete for a younger person's role. I would not consider J. W. the best actor of all time. However, the Western vehicle was the best suited for his demeanor. He was a man's man—not especially handsome according to our classic standards. Yet he was able to ride tall in the saddle.*

Holding company manager, 52, white woman, New York

John Wayne fit the role to a tee. Bad guys always outnumbered him, but he still came through.

Store manager, 63, white man, California

John Wayne earned his only Academy Award for his portrayal of Rooster Cogburn, a quick-on-the-trigger, cantankerous, down-on-his-luck marshal. A drunk, to the point of falling off his horse, with no family, no home, nothing to show for his life except a cot in the corner of a storeroom, Cogburn is described by the town's sheriff as mean, "a pitiless man." At his core, however, he is still John Wayne: formidable, immovable, "double tough," as the Sheriff also describes him, "fear don't enter into his thinking." Chafing under the constraints of law and order, Cogburn is the perfect choice for Mattie Ross (Kim Darby) who is looking for a man who will either kill her father's murderer or see the man hang. "You can't serve papers on a rat," Cogburn observes. "You gotta shoot him or let him be."

Charles Portis, whose novel *True Grit* was published in 1968, had Wayne in mind when he crafted the character and Wayne embraced the one-eyed marshal wholeheartedly. As Wayne told an interviewer:

I knew right away that Rooster Cogburn was a character that fit my pistol. He even felt the same way about life. He did not believe in pampering wrongdoers.

Unafraid to show himself as a fat, aging lawman, or to emphasize Cogburn's imperfections and faults, Wayne brought to the character an unapologetic frankness. He might have been speaking directly to his audience when he tells Mattie, "Baby sister, I was born game and I intend to go out that way." This proudly raucous side, however, is balanced by the affection he develops for his young employer and the quiet moments they share as he relates his not-so-illustrious past, including bank-robbing and an ex-wife who left with his son and a parting shot: "Goodbye Ruben, the love of decency does not abide in you."

In the film's climaxing gunfight, Marshal Cogburn firing two-fisted against four outlaws in a headlong rush on horseback across a mountain meadow, fans are treated to one of the best action sequences Westerns offer. He can't possibly survive, but, of course, he does—without so much as a scratch. With the bad guys vanquished and Mattie saved, *True Grit* ends back at Mattie's ranch in a heartwarming scene at the family cemetery where Mattie offers Rooster a plot next to hers. Thanking her, he asks if it's okay if he doesn't move in anytime soon. With his parting line, "Come see a fat old man sometime," Wayne, in a stunt he performed himself, jumps his horse over a fence, grinning, hat in hand.

Fans delight in John Wayne's portrayal of the aging marshal—the faults, the strength, the indomitable spirit:

> *John Wayne delivered another great performance and he seemed to embody a spirit of the ideals of the Old West, combined with the realistic sacrifices that were made in that era. I admire the spirit of the individuals and animals that possess that special kind of eternal flame or heart that produces "True Grit."*

Field representative, 44, white woman, North Dakota

In all, John Wayne's larger-than-life portrayal, the fall foliage, imposing mountains and quiet valleys, pristine rivers, clean crisp air, a great supporting cast, including Strother Martin, Robert Duvall, and Dennis Hopper (in a minor role) place *True Grit* among many fans' top Westerns.

I love True Grit *for John Wayne. He is a really good actor. The storyline is believable, good believable gunfight scenes.*

Data specialist in electronics manufacturing, 37, white woman, New York

The story was great, the setting was fantastic, the characters were very real personalities. It was slick and smooth. Civil War connection was excellent. It had Texas Rangers and U.S. Marshals.

Professional driver/auto parts, 49, white man, New Jersey

John Wayne as Marshal Rooster Cogburn in *True Grit* (1969), courtesy Photofest

I like Kevin Costner as an actor and I like the character he portrayed, a man who wanted to see the frontier before it was gone; a man with preconceived ideas about Indians; and a man who fell in love! The Native Americans were portrayed as sensitive human beings. Also, the cinematography was so vibrant. I felt I could step into the movie screen and become part of the movie.

Administrative assistant, 54, black woman, Illinois

Dances with Wolves is my favorite for the portrayal of the lonesomeness of the cavalry officer and the extreme fairness to the Indians. The fact that honest-to-God Indians were employed as main characters, extras, AND advisors to assure correctness in the film, along with a real location, as opposed to a set stage, makes this movie just "feel right" to me. The fact that this film was made as it was may just be attributable to Hollywood's sudden compliance to political correctness, but I hope it came about because of an understanding that Indians need to be shown as human, like the rest of us.

Small business co-owner, 60, white woman, New York

Kevin Costner as Lt. John J. Dunbar in *Dances with Wolves* (1990), courtesy Photofest

#6/7 DANCES WITH WOLVES
(1990)

When *Dances with Wolves* (tied for sixth place with *True Grit*) was released in 1990, it was enormously popular across a wide spectrum of people and many reviewers hailed it as a triumph. It had been predicted to be a massive box office flop, however, with Hollywood insiders referring to it as "Kevin's Gate," a derisive reference to Michael Cimino's financial disaster, *Heaven's Gate*, just ten years before. Westerns, since the mid-1970s, had been considered box office poison and, clocking in at three hours, *Dances with Wolves* would be too long for audiences to sit through, or so said conventional wisdom. Worse, the movie focused on Indians (considered an overly romanticized subject), used Native American actors (who purportedly couldn't play convincing characters), and relied on subtitles (which, it was believed, audiences wouldn't tolerate)—three glaring problems, one more problematic than the next. Finally, it featured a first-time director with the audacity to star in his own film. By all industry standards, it should have failed miserably. Seven Academy Awards later, however, including best picture (the first Western to have won the

coveted award since 1931's *Cimarron*), best director, and awards for writing, cinematography, sound, music, and editing, *Dances with Wolves* entered the annals of filmmaking as one of the most successful Westerns ever made.

Dances with Wolves chronicles the experiences of a disillusioned Union Civil War officer reassigned to a remote frontier fort in South Dakota in 1864. Costner's character, Lt. John J. Dunbar, is searching to escape the horror and futility of the "slaughter in the east" and requests to be posted out west "to see the frontier before it's gone." Once there, his fort deserted and finding himself the lone man in charge of maintaining the U.S. Army presence in a far-flung corner of Dakota territory, he comes into contact with a nearby band of Lakota Sioux. In no position to fight, his initial attempts at communication develop into a mutual respect and he is gradually assimilated into the tribe. Spectacular landscapes and a lavish film score serve as backdrop for an exploration of the white man's impact on native cultures on America's far western frontier.

Fans love *Dances with Wolves* for its realism—in this case, what they feel is an accurate portrayal of Native American life:

A very authentic and believable movie. The nomadic life and the coexistence with the land that Native Americans had and portrayed on the screen brought it to life. Using subtitles to retain the original Lakota

It portrays the Indian as a human being and not the stupid savage usually shown in history.

Retired police officer, 61, Native American man, Arizona

Dances with Wolves was beautifully photographed, lots of historically accurate detail (use of Lakota language, for example), not as one-sided in perspective as many films. Hit on a personally favorite theme—seeing the Old West and plains culture before it died. A thing I've always wanted to do.

Administrative assistant for county government, 53, white woman, Minnesota

Kevin Costner and Graham Greene in *Dances with Wolves* (1990), courtesy Photofest

Watching this movie brings up a profound sadness for what has been lost, but joy that it ever existed.

Service area coordinator, 53, white woman, California

This movie brings up sadness, loneliness, a sense of wanting to belong, fit in with the world. The vastness of the world and creation and what a small part of it we really are. Friendliness between cultures. Learning to understand each other and respect other ways. I could sit through this movie again and again, no problem.

Printing company manager, 40, white man, Missouri

Mary McDonnell as Stands With A Fist in *Dances with Wolves* (1990), courtesy Photofest

Sioux language made the film seem more realistic. Filming on location and the exciting buffalo hunt with real buffalo stampeding added to the realism of the story. Every time I view the film, I am overcome by sheer emotion. Pride in my love of the Western epic and total sympathy for all the wrong-doings and betrayals the U.S. government did to the American Indians. During the final closing scenes of the movie, I always choke up and shed tears over the departure and good-bye of Lt. Dunbar and his Indian wife to his Sioux (Lakota) friends.

Supermarket manager, 65, white man, Tennessee

It comes as close to the truth of how this country was "won" in a long time. When I think of freedom, I think of Crazy Horse, or of times before him of Chief Joseph, Tecumseh, Powhattan, and even Massasoit.

Lab technician, 47, Native American man, Rhode Island

Many feel *Dances with Wolves*, with its multifaceted and detail-rich presentation of Lakota cultural life, marks a distinct departure from the stereotypic Hollywood Indian. With Native American actors speaking their dialogue in the Lakota language, the Sioux celebrate victory and love, suffer loss, form deep friendships, and demonstrate loyalty, honor, and courage. In one of the most spectacular segments of the film, warriors on bareback ride through a stampeding herd of buffalo, bringing down huge beasts with arrows and spears in a breathlessly exciting reenactment of the hunt that dramatizes the central importance of the buffalo to Plains cultures. Determined to learn as much about the wasichu (white man) as possible, the Sioux talk and counsel among themselves, strive to comprehend how the coming of whites will change their lives, and gradually accept this white man (Costner) as a valued member of their community.

Dances with Wolves, with its portrayal of Native American culture and a hero who makes the "right" choices by siding with the Indians, touches a nerve among fans—raw, emotional, a mixture of guilt and shame, sadness, longing, and loss, but also pride, triumph of good over evil, and joy. Those who love this movie feel immersed in the frontier of their imagination—a world of understanding, freedom, beauty, personal courage, and rich cultural interaction.

#5 LONESOME DOVE (1989)

From left to right, Robert Duvall and Tommy Lee Jones in *Lonesome Dove* (1989), courtesy Photofest

Number five on the top ten favorite Westerns list, *Lonesome Dove* (a made-for-TV miniseries) also elicits high praise from fans for realism, but here because of its rugged representation of life on the range. Based on Larry McMurtry's 1996 Pulitzer Prize-winning novel of the same name, *Lonesome Dove* tells the story of two former Texas Rangers struggling to

From left to right, Anjelica Huston and Robert Duvall in *Lonesome Dove* (1989), courtesy Photofest

make a go of a cattle company located near a dusty, arid town on the bank of the Rio Grande. The action unfolds as they pick up stakes and drive their herd 2,500 miles to Montana to establish the first cattle ranch that far north. Along the way, they encounter outlaws, horse thieves, Indian raiders, and all manner of disasters, from stampedes to storms to droughts to poisonous snakes.

Lonesome Dove presents a cast of characters who reach deep down and find the strength necessary not only to survive, but to do so while remaining true to themselves. Tommy Lee Jones's Woodrow Call and Robert Duvall's Gus McCrae are adventurers at heart, embracing a high-risk opportunity for the promise it holds out. With honor and integrity, they live life on their own terms. They will never abandon those they care for, nor will they stand by while someone is mistreated.

Gus McCrae, the jokester, loves life and embraces every opportunity to enjoy himself, whether chasing buffalo, gambling, drinking, or having sex—"The older the violin, the sweeter the music," he is fond of saying. Woodrow Call, by contrast, sees life in black-and-white terms and is so self-restrained he can't even verbally acknowledge his own son. But he fights aggressively against wrongdoing, to the point of almost killing a man beating young Newt (Rick Schroder), and fiercely stands by his word, nearly losing his life in fulfilling his promise to a dying Gus to transport Gus's body back to Texas.

The experiences *Lonesome Dove* characters undertake and endure (there are 89 speaking roles) are far from ours, but their emotions, aspirations, and high personal standards resonate strongly with many fans. They struggle, fight, and press on toward goals, large and small—to seek their fortunes, to track down family, to see open country "before all the lawyers and bankers get it," to rekindle old love. They don't mince words, but tell a plain and simple truth. Clara Allen (Anjelica Huston), a pioneer woman in Nebraska and Gus's old flame, does her work and her husband's, too (he is bedridden after having been kicked in the head by a horse). Having seen her share of heartache (losing Gus, three sons, and her husband), she is independent, outspoken, and straightforward—every inch the powerful frontier woman. "You ain't nailed down," she says to July Johnson (Chris Cooper), looking to hire him on to her Nebraska horse ranch even though he's never been out of Arkansas and knows nothing of ranching. "You ain't stupid. You can learn, can't you?"

In the midst of loss and death, there is humor, depth of emotion, courage, honor, and appreciation for the simple things in life. "The only healthy way to live as I see it," Gus advises, "is to learn to like all the little everyday things: a sip of good whiskey of an evening, or a soft bed, or a glass of buttermilk."

Lonesome Dove *comes closest to depicting the real American Cowboy. Spirit of adventure, courage, etc.*

    Judge, 63, white man, Georgia

Lonesome Dove *took ordinary, everyday people of that era and presented love, hate, all the emotions we all feel. It presented a real hero—a loving, caring hero. He wasn't perfect by any means, and everyone didn't always agree with him, but they loved him. Gus was the Old West. His dreams were realistic; his living was forceful, yet careful; and his dying was nothing short of heroic—he chose his own destiny.*

    Bookkeeper, 54, white woman, Mississippi

It brings out the fact that our everyday lives are hectic by our choosing (as a society), and that we can always pick up and make changes. A sense of belonging is there based on the basic values outlined in this Western.

    Programmer/analyst, 36, white woman, Florida

Lonesome Dove *is my favorite because of the horsemanship and the close attention to authenticity of the era.*

    Electrician, 42, Native American man, Colorado

From left to right, Danny Glover, Tim Scott, and Rick Schroder in *Lonesome Dove* (1989), courtesy Photofest

I like that Gus is an older cowboy. The reality of it.

Truck driver, 61, black man, Mississippi

I like to see a man (cowboy) who can put in a "hard day's work" and still be gentle with a woman. This is the kind of life I love—cowboy style, Western, ranching, cattle, land, hardships, a way of life.

Rancher/nurse/volunteer, 48, white woman, Montana

For fans of this Emmy award-winning miniseries, *Lonesome Dove* captures the essence of the Western experience—dirty, hard work on the edge of subsistence, insufferable boredom, but always the opportunity to improve your life, assuming you are willing to take the risks and marshal the perseverance and strength of body and mind to succeed.

Lonesome Dove *seems very real. It shows a lot of aspects of the West such as the women and the choices they were forced to make; dull, boring life in the West, the law, the Indians, cattle drives, life-death. I think it showed it all.*

Teacher, 36, white woman, Rhode Island

To me, at least, it makes some effort to portray the real West. No fancy outfits, dust, scroungy dirty people, hanging of Jake. The West

is glamorized so sometimes the real things aren't there that were the West. Hardship, dirt, lonesomeness, poorly educated people.

Services manager, 62, white woman, Nebraska

The realistic sets and clothing, clipped and colorful dialogue, dry and arid landscape, heartbreaking losses, brutality, but also tenderness and forthright, simple living make many feel *Lonesome Dove* takes them out of the modern world and into the Old West.

#4 THE GOOD, THE BAD AND THE UGLY (1966)

One attribute bringing fans to Western after Western is the gunplay. Suspense and riveting action sequences keep audiences on the edge of their seats and coming back for more. The number four Western on the

Realistic. Human basic instincts. Historical backdrop, scenery, animals. Survival. We watch it over and over and will continue to do so. Each time we see it, we are entertained and enriched.

Retired Veterans Administration hospital worker, 65, white woman, South Dakota

Clint Eastwood as Blondie in *The Good, the Bad and the Ugly* (1966), courtesy Photofest

top favorites list, *The Good, the Bad and the Ugly*, the third film in Italian director Sergio Leone's No Name trilogy, is a good example. There is no dialogue for the first ten minutes of this film, which relies instead on gunfights, narrow escapes, and bounty killings for setup and early development. Against the backdrop of the Civil War, *The Good, the Bad and the Ugly* features three gunmen searching for a horde of Confederate gold. The "good," the "bad," and the "ugly" are only good, bad, and ugly on a relative basis, however; there are no traditional Western heroes here.

Clint Eastwood (as Blondie the "good") and Eli Wallach (as Tuco the "ugly") establish an uneasy partnership early on: Blondie turns Tuco in to local sheriffs in small towns, collects the reward, then shoots the hangman's rope before Tuco is executed and rescues him. The two split the money, but the relationship is based on mutual convenience, never loyalty or trust:

> "The next time I want more than half."
>
> "You cut down my percentage, liable to interfere with my aim."
>
> "But if you miss, then you had better miss very well. Whoever double-crosses me and leaves me alive, he understands nothing about Tuco. Nothing."
>
> Eli Wallach and Clint Eastwood

After exchanging double-crosses, the two come to a precarious alliance as they hunt for the gold—Tuco knows the name of the cemetery, Blondie the name on the grave where the gold is buried. Thrown into the mix is bounty hunter Angel Eyes (Lee Van Cleef as the "bad"), a vicious mercenary. Toward the end of the film, the three meet at the cemetary in an arena-style shootout. Positioned triangularly, the camera lingering on squints, stares, rigid postures, hands moving slowly toward guns, Blondie kills Angel Eyes. At the end of the film, with the gold successfully recovered, Blondie leaves Tuco standing precariously on a gravestone with a hangman's noose around his neck. When Blondie is sufficiently far away, he turns, shoots the rope, and leaves Tuco face down on his pile of gold.

In 1964, when Clint Eastwood was offered the No Name role in the first of Leone's trilogy, *A Fistful of Dollars*, he welcomed the chance to

---

Great talent of Clint Eastwood and the other actors was unforgettable. And the music was very good. I like the history. The way it was—lawlessness.

Commercial construction worker, 33, Latino

The gunfight at the end, the actors. I like Clint Eastwood—his macho personality, the con game that they played.

Mechanic, 65, man

The action is awesome, the plot. I like Clint Eastwood's posture.

Real estate agent, 32, white man, California

I like the acting of Clint Eastwood. The last scene, all three actors, they are standing and pointing guns at each other, the music was good, the tune behind that scene.

Telecommunications engineer, 24, Asian man

From left to right, Eli Wallach and Clint Eastwood, *The Good, the Bad and the Ugly* (1966), courtesy Photofest

play against type. Costarring as Rowdy Yates in television's *Rawhide* gave Eastwood the opportunity to hone his craft, but he soon tired of playing such a conventional role and, as noted in the previous chapter, longed to inject a different quality into his characters. But in the early 1960s, Hollywood wouldn't take such risks, particularly since the Hays Office rules were still in force, which, among other things, didn't allow film-makers to show Western heroes draw until drawn upon or show shoot-out antagonists in the same shot (the camera could either be on one or the other, but never both together). Leone, however, was not subject to those rules and when Eastwood, ever restive, ever the risk-taker, read the

From left to right, Lee Van Cleef, Eli Wallach, and Clint Eastwood, *The Good, the Bad and the Ugly* (1966), courtesy Photofest

The Good, the Bad and the Ugly had a haunting movie theme and the theme of good and evil was up-front. It had the excitement of risk-taking and winning. Clint Eastwood has made several Western movies and this one is the best of them. It pictures the hero alone fighting the odds and winning.

Retired teacher, 61, Latino woman, Texas

The Good, the Bad and the Ugly is the one that got me hooked on Westerns. I liked the comedy in it, the drama, also there was horror, murder, etc. That movie consisted of everything. I liked the history in it. There was a realness to it.

Factory worker, 41, white woman, Kentucky

script, he took the job; he was looking to play the Western hero just as Leone envisioned it. As Eastwood described himself to one interviewer:

> There's a rebel lying deep in my soul. Anytime anybody tells me the trend is such and such, I go the opposite direction. I hate the idea of trends. I hate imitation; I have a reverence for individuality. I got where I am by coming off the wall.

Although *A Fistful of Dollars* had a marginal chance of success, the risk wasn't all that high for Eastwood. In addition to a $15,000 paycheck, he could travel to Europe, visiting a part of the world he hadn't been to before; he could be exposed to how other people made films—his interest in directing developed early on; and if the film flopped, no one in the States would see it, so it wouldn't damage his career. As it turned out, the film was a hit in its native Italy and throughout Europe, as was its sequel, *For A Few Dollars More,* made the following year (1965). In 1967, when United Artists saw how well the films had done in Europe, the studio optioned distribution rights and marketed the films, including the third in the trilogy, *The Good, the Bad and the Ugly,* in the United States.

Leone's trilogy signaled a change in Westerns—but not one welcomed by all. *New York Times* reviewer Renata Adler commented of *The Good, the Bad and the Ugly*, "Anyone who would voluntarily remain in the theater to see this movie in its entirety (while he might be a mild, sweet person in his private life) is not someone I should want to meet, in any capacity, ever." But many Western fans enjoy the grittiness introduced to the genre with this series of Westerns. Leone crafted a highly stylized look—a harsh, blistering quality. The plot is thin; *The Good, the Bad and the Ugly* does not have a strong story. But the movie is popular for its action and style—the "look" (Clint Eastwood throwing his poncho over his shoulder), Ennio Morricone's haunting score, the cigar, the sweat, the

Lee Van Cleef as Angel Eyes in *The Good, the Bad and the Ugly* (1966), courtesy Photofest

squint, the gunfire. For many Western fans, *The Good, the Bad and the Ugly* shows what the Old West was really like: hot, dusty, gritty, uncertain, perilous.

> The Good, the Bad and the Ugly *has haunting music, beautiful scenery, and good acting—a feeling of really being "immersed," so to speak, in the movie. One can almost feel the dust and grime being around you!*
>
> Teacher, 52, white man, Massachusetts

Add to that humor, unexpected plot twists, and three interesting and unique characters—the emotionally minimalist Blondie, the lustily passionate Tuco, the brutally sadistic Angel Eyes—and you have another top fan favorite.

#3 HIGH NOON (1952)

High Noon has a relatively simple plot: A retiring marshal dons the badge one last time to battle a murderer he had sent to prison seven years before, who, newly freed and scheduled to arrive on the noon train, has vowed to kill him. Throughout, Marshal Will Kane (Gary Cooper) struggles in vain to enlist the aid of apathetic and cowardly townspeople who choose to hide rather than stand beside their marshal and defend their community against Miller and his gang. Spanning the real-time 85 minutes the marshal has to ready himself for the climactic gunfight, most of the film takes place within the confines of the town. In what could easily have been reduced to a tiresome cliche, the efforts of producer/screenwriter Carl Foreman, director Fred Zinnemann, cinematographer Floyd Crosby, and composer Dimitri Tiomkin combine to create a timeless film that crackles with tension as the noon hour approaches. *High Noon* is number three on the favorite movie Westerns list.

High Noon was the eighth highest grossing film of 1952. But, like *Dances with Wolves*, number six on the top favorites list, *High Noon*, by all industry standards, should not have been a success. To begin with, it was one of the first "adult" Westerns made, using the genre to explore wider

Gary Cooper as Marshal Will Kane in *High Noon* (1952), courtesy Photofest

I enjoy High Noon *for the mounting tension as the camera keeps showing the clock and Gary Cooper not being able to get anybody to help him. How everyone in town comes up with a reason not to help. How he wrestles with his inner self concerning his duty and honor versus why should he risk death for a town that doesn't seem to care?*

Gas utility construction foreman, 53, white man, Minnesota

issues of violence, alienation, social disintegration and conflict—and this was relatively new for audiences in the early 1950s. But, more specifically, in an era known for reinforcing the status quo, *High Noon* inverted many values fundamental to the genre.

Marshal Kane's requests for aid are rebuffed throughout—the town's judge is packing his belongings (American flag, gavel, law books, symbolic scales of justice) and preparing to run; townspeople avoid the marshal

From left to right, *Gary Cooper and uncredited actor, High Noon* (1952), courtesy Photofest

and point blank refuse assistance when approached in the town's church; a former lawman (and Kane's mentor) tells him "it's all for nothin'." Most notably, at the end of the film, when all four gunmen are dead and the townspeople emerge rather sheepishly from where they have been hiding to gather around their marshal, Kane plucks the badge from his vest and drops it in the dirt at his feet—one of the film's most provocative moments and one that prompted John Wayne to describe *High Noon* as "the most un-American thing I've ever seen in my whole life."

And if the film itself didn't offend audiences, production and historic contexts also made its success questionable. Modestly budgeted, it was in rehearsal for just one week and shot in only one month. It featured a male star (Gary Cooper), ill and aging, on somewhat of a downhill slide, paired with a much younger and unknown costar (Grace Kelly).

In addition, a newly emergent media—television—was beginning to take its toll on box office receipts and the decision to shoot in a grainy black and white went against the common thinking that Technicolor spectaculars were what attracted audiences. (The year *High Noon* was released, 1952, also saw *The Greatest Show on Earth, Quo Vadis,* and *Ivanhoe.*) Most problematic, the film was made at the height of McCarthyism and studio head Stanley Kramer was a noted leftist. Further, before the film was even released, producer/screenwriter Carl Foreman was blacklisted after being called before the House Un-American Activities Committee (HUAC) and declared an uncooperative witness.

Despite the odds against it—a relatively low budget, the questionable bankability of its stars, its deeper psychological explorations, and its political context—*High Noon* triumphed, grossing $3.4 million at the box office, a nice return on an $800,000 investment. It garnered four Academy Awards—best actor, theme song, musical score, editing—and takes its place as one of the finest Westerns ever made.

Western fans enjoy many aspects of this film—the script, music, characterizations, acting. Many also find that the issues explored continue to resonate today—people refusing to stand up against that which they know is wrong, emotional isolation from a seemingly heartless community, the deep personal courage necessary to fight for your beliefs and the right to live life on your own terms.

> *There are everyday principles involved, such as people not wanting to become involved in what should be a community effort to combat that which is wrong. The principle of assisting people is under attack here. The ethics of the situation. It can be seen in real life also.*
>
> Retired probation counselor, 72, white man, Rhode Island

But the primary and ongoing draw of *High Noon* is its broad theme: One man, refusing to run, perseveres despite being nearly completely abandoned by his community. He is clearly afraid, but faces his fear and does what he has to do. As one Western fan notes:

> *We've all had the experience, at one time or another, of being in trouble and going to someone we trust for help only to discover that they don't care. The fact that Will Kane was able to find the strength*

High Noon is a man standing up for his principles when all around him refuse to help.

Chemical plant worker, 60, white man

High Noon is my favorite for the various elements of the story, the conflicts within the hero, all the fears pulling at him.

History and social studies teacher, 58, white man, Minnesota

Although Westerns don't portray my lifestyle as a lesbian, they are still escapist. I love to daydream and escape into the excitement, the fear, knowing I'll walk out in two hours or so. I love the use of the clock in High Noon *depicting how time is passing and the sense of urgency and desperation and resignation Gary Cooper feels with every tick of the clock. Second, I love the storyline— how one individual faces up to evil against all odds, having no illusions about how great and heroic he is, just that he has a job to do and he will do the best he can.*

Electrician, 49, white woman, Rhode Island

High Noon tells a simple story of good overcoming evil despite high odds. It makes sense—it is not pretentious. It makes a very solid statement. It gives me a sense of peace, the feeling that here all can be handled.

Social work volunteer/ homemaker, 80, white woman, Maine

within himself to stand alone against heavy odds serves as a splendid example of what one man can accomplish when he knows that what he has to do is right.

Paramedic, 52, white man, Iowa

Because of this simple, universally applicable theme, a diversity of individuals find personal significance in this film. In fact, it was a favorite of two American presidents with quite different styles and philosophies: Dwight D. Eisenhower and Bill Clinton.

"Standing up for his principles," "the fears pulling at him," does "the right thing regardless of overwhelming odds," "the sense of urgency and desperation and resignation"—these are the attributes fans admire most in Marshal Will Kane.

Gary Cooper stands up to the bad guys because he thinks it is the right thing to do, regardless of the overwhelming odds against him.

Real estate investor, 38, white man, Colorado

High Noon's grainy black-and-white cinematography, nondescript town setting (there is little Western landscape shown in this movie), and fairly

From left to right, Lon Chaney Jr., Gary Cooper, and Grace Kelly, *High Noon* (1952), courtesy Photofest

standard Hollywood Western costumes are not what make this movie "authentic." Rather, it is the situation Marshal Kane faces, his resolve, and his ultimate triumph. *High Noon* explores deeply personal dilemmas: At what point do you take a stand? What battles do you fight? What are your personal limits? How much courage can you muster to do what you think is right? To protect those whom you love most? For many fans, survival in the Old West took someone who could push him/herself to the limits of strength, courage, and endurance. *High Noon* gives them an opportunity to explore that.

#2 THE SEARCHERS (1956)

The heroes in most of the top ten favorites may not be perfect, but they are clearly "good"—the Seven who sacrifice their lives for Mexican villagers, the boozing Marshal Cogburn who brings killers to justice, pleasure-seeking Gus who lives his life with honor and integrity. Not all fans like their heroism served up in black and white terms, however. Some prefer something grittier, something more complex, harder to relate to, harder to like, yet magnetic and compelling. Like William Munny in *Unforgiven*, Ethan Edwards of *The Searchers* pushes the limits of the Western hero.

The Searchers unfolds as Ethan (John Wayne) and his adopted nephew, Martin (Jeffrey Hunter), embark on a journey to find Martin's younger sister Debbie (Lana and Natalie Wood), taken captive during a Comanche raid of the family homestead that left her the lone survivor. Traveling thousands of miles (from Texas to Wyoming), weathering all elements, following up on every lead, time suspends for Ethan and Martin as they focus solely on their quest, foregoing family and creature comforts. The search ends after five years when they find Debbie and bring her home.

Although the plot may sound rather conventional, *The Searchers* is anything but. Unusually stark, the movie is raw and grim. Emotions are on the edge, whether the characters are suffering the pain of unrequited love, harnessing the determination to make a go of it on the frontier, or indulging deep hatreds. The cinematography is vibrant and rich, with oranges, blues,

John Wayne as Ethan Edwards in *The Searchers* (1956), courtesy Photofest

The scenes are very authentic looking—simple, rugged, plain. A lot of interesting characters—Mose Harper, Rev. Sam, Martin Pawley, etc. Depicts the rough reality of living in the West—vast spaces between civilization, danger.

Office manager, 49, white man, Ohio

and reds, contrasting lights and darks, and vivid shadows. Hot wind, dust, and skeletal rock formations piercing the sky complete the visual effects to underscore the film's themes of the precariousness of life and the volatility of emotion.

But what makes *The Searchers* truly unusual, and popular among Western fans, is not so much its plot or cinematography, but its main character. At its heart is a brooding, angry, embittered John Wayne hero. He shares many attributes with the traditional Man of the West—tenacity, persistence, determination, courage, skill, strength—but in many ways he is the antithesis of heroic behavior. He is vicious, shooting retreating Comanche warriors trying to pick up their dead and wounded; he is caustic, treating his nephew with contempt, calling him "blanket-head," "half-breed"; he is bloodthirsty, scalping Comanche chief Scar toward the end of the film. He is filled with rage and race hatred, is bitter, antagonistic, and obsessive.

At first determined to rescue Debbie and bring her home, Ethan's goal changes as the years pass and it becomes clear Debbie is of an age to be sexually involved with her captors. By the middle of the film, he obsessively searches not to rescue but to kill her, miscegenation such a disgrace to her and her family that death is the only option. At the last moment, however, when Ethan finally has his opportunity "to put a bullet in her brain," he looks down at her and, overcoming his hatred, sweeps her into his arms and takes her home. The film ends as Debbie is welcomed back into the community while Ethan himself remains at the door, the perennial outsider, never to be accepted into society.

Fans of *The Searchers* are captivated by what they find to be unusually challenging themes and complex, realistic representations. Hardly the traditional and easily recognizable "good guy," Ethan Edwards is clearly a racist—much of his behavior is questionable, even reprehensible. But he is the hero of the film (and John Wayne), positioned as a leader, a strong, positive force, and fans sympathize with and admire him despite his glaring faults. He perseveres against impossible odds—weather, outlaws, Indians, time. He is unwavering in his pursuit—he will never quit. And in the end, he "does the right thing." By embracing Debbie, many feel, he changes and grows. Despite the many losses in his life, despite his

From left to right, John Wayne, uncredited actress, and Jeffrey Hunter, *The Searchers* (1956), courtesy Photofest

deep-seated hatred, he is able to take his niece into his arms and bring her home. For fans of this Western, it is this depth of character (honor and hatred) that makes *The Searchers* ring true and a perennial favorite:

> *Great combination of Western drama, humor, and adventure, with a central character who is both hateful and heroic, embodying both good and bad qualities of the West—courageous, "frontier-smart," loyal, determined, and also stubborn, intolerant, and racist.*

> Sales executive, 54, white man, New York

> *Ford's subtexts keep me entranced. The comparisons between Ethan Edwards and Chief Scar are fascinating (as they are both very strongly race haters by nature). John Wayne's acting is uncharacteristically excellent (probably because Ford let Wayne act out his own race bias*

The film tackles two of the most important issues in American life (race and miscegenation) without resorting to sensationalism or preachiness. As a symbol to most people, John Wayne represents some sort of mindless "might is right" American vigilantism. Wayne's character, Ethan Edwards, subverts that stereotype by offering a chilling portrait of the viciousness of a predatory outlaw.

Public relations manager, 43, white man, Maryland

John Wayne's portrayal of Ethan Edwards is a standout. The character's complexities are at the center of the film. Ford's use of scenery (Monument Valley), music, color, shadows (particularly the constant framed silhouettes), balanced between comedy, pathos, and tragedy all help to enhance the theme of prejudice. Pretty strong stuff for a Western.

Actor/teacher, 53, white man, Missouri

The character Ethan is so strong, determined, stubborn, and yet right in his beliefs. Doesn't give up easily.

Retired salesman, 69, white man, Indiana

I like the cinematography and location shooting. It relays the grand scope of the land and its vastness. The storyline that dealt with John Wayne's character's hatred toward Indians and how he had to deal with it while trying to rescue his niece. The struggle of his own good and evil sides. And the final shot through the door. WOW!!

Radio announcer, 60, white man, Minnesota

Deals with strong love/ hate moral issues—same as today. It covers all elements of emotions—a rarity. Comes out with a good strong believable ending.

Actor, white man, Michigan

Don't ever quit! This movie could have been about my family. They had similar experiences. Indian raids, violent death. They are still there on the same ranch. We may get down, but we always come back.

Small manufacturing company owner, 59, white man, Texas

The Searchers is my favorite for the powerful emotions it evokes, and how these emotions control our lives.

State trooper, 46, white man, Pennsylvania

Background photo of John Wayne as Ethan Edwards in *The Searchers* (1956), courtesy Photofest

To me, The Searchers is the perfect blend of all that is good in a Western movie. It seems to touch every human emotion I possess. Even today I can remember the way I felt watching that movie.

Retired elementary school teacher, 61, white woman, Iowa

freely and deliberately). Ethan Edwards's subtle and gruff tenderness is generally overlooked by film critics—and he is not the most likeable of individuals—but he does maintain his code of honor to the very end.

Retail salesman, 57, white man, Minnesota

#1 SHANE (1953)

The number one favorite *Shane* has everything Western fans love: good triumphing unconditionally over evil; great action sequences (barroom brawls, fistfights, gunfights); strong, loving families; a community that bands together during a crisis; magnificent landscape; and memorable music. In the character of Shane, it offers a traditional hero—skilled, tenacious, and decisive—who sacrifices himself for the good of the family (or woman) he has come to love. But what makes *Shane* stand apart is not so much that it contains these elements—many Westerns do—or even that it has an unusual plot—its story pitting homesteaders against a ruthless cattle baron is hardly unique. What makes *Shane* stand apart is the exceptional quality of every aspect of this film.

Set against the magnificence of the Grand Tetons, director George Stevens offers a beautifully textured Western that captures the essence of the frontier spirit: strong, determined individuals who struggle against the elements (natural and human) and persevere. From its Academy Award-winning cinematography to the detail paid to clothing, sets, and sound, to the interpersonal relationships explored among the main characters, *Shane* takes its place as one of the all-time classic (and favorite) Westerns.

In the opening of *Shane*, a lone rider approaches a newly built homestead. Though initially met with suspicion, Shane (Alan Ladd) is welcomed into the Starrett family, hiring on to help with the work involved in establishing a viable farm. A gunfighter who knows he has outlived his time, Shane is eager to hang up his guns. Laying aside his wilderness buckskins, he dons workman's clothing and attempts to live a quieter, more stable life. But unable to stand aside while trouble escalates

Shane is my favorite because many moral issues were covered. The fast gun siding with the little ranchers, the interest in the little boy, the respect for the husband concerning his wife, and for Shane putting a hole in Jack Palance!

Retired state liquor store manager, 71, white man, North Carolina

between the community of homesteaders and the local cattle baron, Rufus
Ryker (Emile Meyer), Shane changes back into his buckskins, takes up
his guns once again, and "disposes" of Ryker and two henchmen, including Jack Palance in an early role as gunman Jack Wilson. Shane rides off

Alan Ladd in the title role, *Shane* (1953), courtesy Photofest

The story is beautiful in its simplicity, with each character skillfully portraying people we know were real. The gunfighter running from his past, but inevitably having to confront it. He sacrifices his own desires for a happy life to destroy evil (Jack Palance) that could ruin the lives of so many of the solid citizens who do not have the killer instinct to do it themselves.

Letter carrier, 50, white man, Arizona

wounded at the end of the film as the small boy, Joey Starrett (played by Brandon De Wilde), who has watched him with adulation throughout, cries plaintively, "Come back, Shane. Shane, come back."

When Western fans describe what they enjoy about *Shane*, "realism" and "believability" top the list, particularly with respect to the characterizations, settings, and vision of pioneer life:

Shane shows what life was like then. Building a cabin. Living a simple and (morally) clean life. Getting together with friends and neighbors for festival occasions, no matter how few in number per year.

Retired computer systems information professor, 66, white man, Massachusetts

When identifying with the heroine, it makes me feel protected to see the protagonist protect his woman and fight to keep her safe.

Newspaper writer/ photographer, 65, white woman, California

Shane is the mysterious stranger.

Structural engineer, 53, Latino man, New Mexico

The hero is against great odds but finds a way to overcome the evil or bad ones.

Minister, 70, white man, Tennessee

I enjoy the story, a man who didn't answer to anyone because he was fast enough and rough enough that no one dared question him. But he was also gentle enough to help others who were not of his breed.

Dealer, 68, white man, New Jersey

Opposite from left to right, Alan Ladd and Brandon De Wilde in *Shane* (1953), courtesy Photofest

It's not so much that Shane is different. It just does everything so well. It's very believable.

Technical writer, 50, white man, New Jersey

Each makes you believe in the part he's playing as if they really were these people.

Dressmaker, 60, black woman, Kentucky

As with many Westerns, the evocation of America's pioneer spirit and sense of community garners specific praise:

Shane makes me feel pride in my family's frontier past—nostalgia for harder but in many ways better times.

Retired schoolteacher and administrator, 68, white man, Rhode Island

Some, both men and women, also enjoy the depiction of a traditional family environment—cozy cabins with clearly defined gender roles, "where men were men and women were women."

Makes me feel that the man is in charge and he loves his woman deeply and really will protect and cherish her.

Customer service representative, 53, white woman, Ohio

When watching Shane, I feel transported to a different world where men were men and the ladies were respected.

31, white man, Maryland

But the biggest reason fans love *Shane* is because of the character of Shane himself. Shane is in every respect a traditional Western hero. He is a loner and we know nothing of his past, except that he is a gunfighter. He picks his fights carefully and only after extreme provocation, dispatching his adversaries with skill and speed. A chivalrous champion of the homesteaders' cause, he befriends Joey and does not take advantage of the affections of Marian Starrett (Jean Arthur). Known only as "Shane," he has no specific identity and his future is at best tenuous, the perennial outsider riding off wounded at the end of the film, anonymity deliberately highlighted by his bowed head, concealing his face as he

rides toward an uncertain fate. In his plight, a man searching for a new life because there is no longer a place for "his kind," he garners audience sympathy and affection.

"Your days are over," he warns Ryker.

"Mine?" is the reply. "What about yours, gunslinger?" A silence reveals Shane's acknowledgement. "Difference is," Shane finally replies, "I know it." But Shane comes to realize he cannot change and, in this realization, comes to accept himself: "A man has to be what he is, Joey. Can't break the mold. I tried and I couldn't."

Audiences are drawn to the fact that even though Shane cannot change, it is in being himself that he saves the community. The message: An individual, true to him/herself, acting with honor, integrity, and courage will prevail.

> Shane *shows the essential human drama of a man trying to live down a past that is not entirely his fault, but which nonetheless continues to affect his life. The past does NOT in fact equal the future, yet many times our acquaintances continue to judge us by circumstances not entirely under our control. In spite of his dark past, Shane does an enormous amount of good for the family who hires him before being forced to move on. Shane embodies a substantial grace under enormous pressure, an admirable trait in my opinion.*
>
>   Market research interviewer, 52, white woman, Arkansas

Being true to himself comes with a price, however: foregoing his dreams and being forever alienated from the woman and the world he has just made safe. As with *The Magnificent Seven*, fans are drawn to this notion of sacrifice, many wondering if they would do the same:

> *I'm fascinated by the idea of the lone, strong hero. The idea of sacrifice. It's really what a hero is all about. If you're not sacrificing anything, you're just in it for your own self-aggrandizement. You have empathy for Shane, for any kind of decision you might want to make in your life where you might have to sacrifice something.*
>
>   Technical writer, 50, white man, New Jersey

I am a sucker for good triumphing over evil. Shane has character—he shows who he is and what he's all about. It makes me wonder if I have the courage to stand up for what is right.

Stockbroker, 63, white man, Massachusetts

Shane elicits a variety of emotions in fans. On the one hand, the mounting tension and ultimate triumph is thrilling:

Struggle of good against evil. Sexy shootout scene!

Medical seminar coordinator, 64, white woman, New York

And yet there is also a sense of loss—loss of innocence, loss of a way of life, loss of a romanticized era in our history:

Ladd's character is the Old West. Joey's echoing cry is ours, too: "Shane, come back! Come back, Shane!"

Retired controller's assistant, 65, white man, New Jersey

The delineation of heroism, combined with the suspense and action, innocence and loss, fear and perseverance draws many different kinds of people to *Shane* and makes it stand out as an all-time favorite movie Western.

Calling for Shane at the end tugs your heart. He survived the gun battle, then goes off. He didn't get anything he started out for. Didn't get his new life, didn't get the girl. Did accomplish saving the livelihood of his new friends, but lost his chance at a new life.

Public affairs clerk, white man, Wisconsin

Tremendously sad, very sad at the end. When you're small, sometimes you identify with people in the news, actors, heroes, and you lose them at some point and you lose your youth at the same time. His loss is our loss, too.

Technical writer, 50, white man, New Jersey.

A Final Word on Favorite Westerns

From left to right, John Dierkes, Emile Meyer, and Jack Palance in *Shane* (1953), courtesy Photofest

If *your* particular favorite is not among the top ten favorite Westerns cited here, do not be disheartened. There are certainly Western fans who would put one or more of these movies as among their *least* favorite. Hear this fan on the number one favorite, *Shane*:

> *Shane is a classic, but I have problems with it. The theme as I see it is that suburban values triumph over the individual. At the beginning, Ryker with his beard blowing in the wind gives his "I'm a reasonable man, but" speech. Whether he had a right to take the land from the Indians is another issue, but it is now being overrun by suburbanites. My personal problem with this picture is that I liked Ryker and wanted him to run these squatters off his land. I thought he was a reasonable man. He gave the squatters ample time to git, but they wouldn't budge. And what makes this movie more disturbing is that the theme came true. Suburban sprawl won out and the Rykers of this country are gone. It's obviously evident that I'd rather sit around the saloon with Ryker and Wilson than go to a bean supper with the homesteaders.*
>
> Library worker, 65, white man, Rhode Island

149

From left to right, Ben Johnson, Warren Oates, William Holden, and Ernest Borgnine in *The Wild Bunch* (1969), courtesy Photofest

I saw The Wild Bunch *prior to my going to Vietnam. I thought I'd never see my parents and friends again, so this movie reminds me of a time in my youth when I had to be strong.*

Elementary school teacher, 59, white man, Connecticut

Of the 1,052 Western fans interviewed, *Shane* tops the list by being the favorite for only 5%. Number ten, *Unforgiven*, is the number one favorite for only 2%. These numbers are so low because, as noted previously, these 1,052 Western fans cited over 100 different Westerns as their favorites. Why so many movies?

First, of course, there are many Westerns to choose from. About 25% to 30% of films produced by major and independent studios from 1926 to 1959 were Westerns, with the genre comprising at least 10% to 20% of total movie output in each of the next ten years—thousands of Westerns have been made throughout filmmaking history. These movies, though all Westerns, are enormously diverse. Many tell similar types of stories (tales of wagon trains, cattle drives, pioneer struggles, frontier town development) with a similar range of characters (lawmen, outlaws, Indians, ranchers, homesteaders, cowboys, drifters, saloon denizens) in a similar geographic setting (canyons, deserts, grassy plains, mountains). But how these elements are put together, how the themes are explored, how an individual struggle is portrayed, how heroism is defined—these give the genre a tremendous breadth.

Second, the audience is highly diverse. Preferences are influenced by a variety of attributes and circumstances, among them generational differences (people tend to enjoy movies that were popular in their youths) and gender and racial differences (women and whites are more likely to favor John Wayne over Clint Eastwood, whereas men and people of color tend to like them both equally). There are also preferences reflecting diverse backgrounds, life experiences, and points of view—urban versus rural upbringing, family history, military experience, political beliefs, just plain personal taste.

True Grit is my favorite for John Wayne, of course! Also, it is a more contemporary film. Wonderful cinematography and great music. I remember living in California when it was released. My friends and I saw it several times at the movie theatre and seeing that particular movie reminds me of that time and place.

Program administrator, 49, white woman, Rhode Island

Every time I view my favorite, Rio Bravo (and I do frequently), I get the same feeling—like visiting old friends, enjoying them, sharing their trials and tribulations, their defeats, and ultimate victory. I was eight years old when I first saw it, and I feel the same way now as I did then. It may not be the best Western, but it fills a special place in my heart.

Actor/teacher, 53, white man, Missouri

From left to right, John Wayne, Dean Martin, Rick Nelson, and Angie Dickenson in *Rio Bravo* (1959), courtesy Photofest

Finally, there are so many favorite movie Westerns because favorites are emotional choices—highly personal and subjective. A favorite Western has an emotional pull. It can remind fans of a specific time in their lives, comfort or move them, validate a specific point of view, or simply take them out of their everyday lives through some rip-snortin' entertainment. This contrasts with what people might consider the "best" Western, which might be judged on more standardized criteria: production values (e.g., cinematography, acting, script, direction), historical context in which the film was released (e.g., *High Noon* and McCarthyism, *The Searchers* and racial equality, *The Wild Bunch* and Vietnam-era disillusionment), or the role a particular movie played in furthering the genre (e.g., inverting, challenging, or changing standardized characterizations or themes—the adult or psychological Western of the 1950s, the antihero of the 1960s). One fan, for example, cites *Wagon Master* (1950) as her favorite:

> *With no big stars, it hits all the right buttons. It calls up in me feelings of jealousy, longing, envy, and sadness. I would have loved to have been there. Part of me would give anything I own to go back and experience the trip west. However, another part of me, the part that likes indoor toilets and air conditioning, that part says "forget it, girl"!*
>
> Medical staff assistant, 53, white woman, Florida

She deems *The Searchers* (1956), however, to be the best Western ever made, but a movie she does not enjoy watching:

> *John Ford and John Wayne, an unbeatable team. This Western addresses important issues, not the least of which is racism. It's not my favorite, however, because of the very dark overtones. I find it depressing—especially the fact that Ethan is still the loner, still the outsider at the end of the film. It has the script, the acting, the director, the locale, and the cinematography that earned it the title "best."*

In another five to ten years, the favorite Westerns list could look quite different. It is a product of the era in which the survey was taken, the age of the fan base, and how we interpret history. How will we look at the Old West several years from now? What will resonate as "believable"? What issues will be important to us? How will we want to see our heroes?

From left to right, Gene Wilder and Cleavon Little in *Blazing Saddles* (1974), courtesy Photofest

Will the "revisionist" Westerns of the 1990s still draw audiences? What new Westerns will we have to choose from?

One thing is certain, however. With such a continual and strong following, with Westerns available on television and video/DVD, with new Westerns being made, and new generations of Western fans coming to the genre (through parents, grandparents, other family members, or simply on their own), saddle up, pardners—the Western is alive and well.

If you would like to share your opinions and thoughts about Westerns with the author, copy and fill out the questionnaire in Appendix C and send it to:

Maverick Spirit Press

I Love Westerns

P.O. Box 113

Manville, RI 02838

You can also take the survey online at

www.ilovewesterns.com/questionnaire

Your comments may be used anonymously in future

editions of this book.

APPENDIX A

RESEARCH METHODOLOGY

The interviews with Western fans conducted for this book were done in two phases. The first was in 1994. In this phase, respondents were recruited through local newspapers and Western film festivals. To begin, I sent a press release describing preliminary findings gleaned from books, articles, and casual conversations to over 600 entertainment editors of U.S. newspapers (see Appendix B for the text of the press release and a list of the newspapers that carried it). I know of at least 45 newspapers from Alaska and Oregon to Maine and Florida that printed word of the survey between mid-April and October 1994. Short articles publicized the survey and invited readers to participate by writing to me care of "I Love Westerns" for a questionnaire.

Questionnaire responses were anonymous in order to assure participants' privacy as well as free them to express their opinions. People sent letters requesting survey materials and, in return, were sent a cover letter thanking them for their participation (and notifying them that their responses could be used in publications), a questionnaire, and a self-addressed, stamped return envelope. No record of who received which questionnaire was kept (questionnaires weren't numbered until they came in); postmarks indicated area of origin, but there were no other identifiers. One participant commented that he couldn't see how results could be trusted since, in not identifying themselves, people were not "accountable" for their responses. But it was precisely the assurance of anonymity that freed many people to speak their minds, from a thirty year old white man in Mississippi who insisted "freeing the slaves was the worst thing we ever did" to several others who revealed painful personal histories (alcoholic parents, troubled families).

It was from a participant in Mississippi that I learned of the many Western film festivals held around the country each year. I attended four: a B Western festival in Knoxville, Tennessee, May 12–14; a John Wayne Film Fest in Akron, Ohio, June 10–12; a Wild West Weekend in Sonora, California, September 23–25; and a Western film conference at the Buffalo Bill Historical Center in Cody, Wyoming, November 4–5. I talked to fans and handed out questionnaires at all these events.

Between people who heard of the survey via newspaper articles and those at the Western film festivals, I collected 552 completed questionnaires in 1994 (see Appendix C for the 1994 survey). I limited my investigation to movie Westerns (rather than TV and novel forms) to narrow the field of focus (the made-for-television miniseries *Lonesome Dove* was so popular among fans, however, I included it). Respondents were *not* prompted with lists of movies or top reasons why they might enjoy Westerns. Once questionnaires were collected, I coded and analyzed results. The original 1994 survey was not designed to quantify the Western audience, either to provide a statistic of Western fans as a percentage of the U.S. adult population or to profile the Western audience itself.

In the summer of 2003, I updated the 1994 research with a random digit dial telephone survey (i.e., telephone numbers from a database were dialed by a computer at random). I purchased 21,000 phone numbers from a large database of working residential telephone exchanges in the United States. Numbers were generated at random to represent U.S. household density across the nation (e.g., more numbers were generated in California than Montana because population density is higher in California). No other criteria were imposed on the sample—it was completely random. A total of 500 Western fans (identified through a screening process described below) were interviewed by an independent telephone survey house. Statistics reported in this book are from this phase of the research alone, with a sampling error of +/-3% or 4% (depending on sample size). *The only exception is the top ten favorite Westerns list*. I combined the movies named as favorites from both pieces of research. Because so many movies were mentioned, results are stronger using the combined samples. This list is *not* statistically representative, however; it merely indicates top favorites.

The telephone survey was somewhat shorter than the 1994 questionnaire and took 10 to 12 minutes to complete. Open-ended responses were coded after they were gathered. Respondents qualified for the survey on the basis of *one* qualification alone—they were required to answer a "4" or a "5" on a five-point scale to the question "How much would you say you enjoy watching Western movies, whether in your home watching on television or a video/DVD, or in the theater? Please use a scale of one to five, where one is not at all, and five is very." There were no other sampling requirements; respondent demographics (e.g., gender, age, race, occupation) were allowed to fall naturally; there were no quotas set for the number of interviews among men or women, those in specific age or racial groups, specific occupations, etc.

In order to find 500 Western fans, 1,677 people were screened (not everyone loves Westerns). Respondents were asked demographic information (gender, age, race) and then the qualification question ("How much would you say you enjoy watching Western movies, whether in your home watching on television or a video/DVD, or in a theater?"). Of the 1,677 contacted to participate in the telephone survey research, 500 (or 30%) qualified, answering "4" or "5" on a five-point scale to how much they enjoy watching movie Westerns. This means approximately 30% (+/-3%) of the U.S. population *today* enjoys watching Westerns (500 of 1,677 people said they enjoy watching Westerns, or 29.8%).

The following table (Figure 1) shows the percent of people who enjoy watching Westerns by specific subgroups, notably gender, age, and race. Findings show men enjoy watching Westerns at a rate of about twice that of women, and older people are more likely to be Western fans (e.g.,

13% of people age 18–34, but 45% of those 65 and older enjoy watching Westerns). In terms of race, however, interest is the same: 30% of whites and 29% of people of color are Western fans.

+/- 3% margin of error

Demographics	% WHO ENJOY WESTERNS N=1,677
Gender	
Men	41%
Women	23%
Age	
18–34	13%
35–44	27%
45–64	35%
65+	45%
Race	
White	30%
People of color	29%

FIGURE 1. BREAKDOWN OF WESTERN FANS AS PERCENT OF U.S. POPULATION

Figure 2 below compares the final sample of 500 Western fans with U.S. 2000 Census data. With the exception of gender and age, the Western audience is remarkably representative. The U.S. population is 75% white and 25% people of color, whereas the Western audience is 79% white and 21% people of color (+/-4%). Western fans are found in all regions of the country, in alignment with the distribution of the U.S. population (e.g., 19% of people in the U.S. live in the northeast, 16% of Western fans live in the northeast). Educationally, Western fans are an exact match to the U.S. population (76% have completed up through two years of college, 24% have a bachelor's degree or higher). Annual household income is comparable.

DEMOGRAPHICS	U.S. 2000 CENSUS	WESTERN FANS N = 500
Gender		
Men	49%	63%
Women	51%	37%
Age		
18–34	29%	12%
35–44	22%	17%
45–64	31%	42%
65+	18%	29%
Race		
White	75%	79%
People of color	25%	21%
Region		
Northeast	19%	16%
South	36%	38%
Midwest	23%	28%
West	22%	19%
Education		
Up through 2 years of college	76%	76%
Bachelor's degree or higher	24%	24%
Annual HH Income		
<$50 K	58%	63%
>$50 K	42%	37%

+/- 4% margin of error

FIGURE 2. COMPARING WESTERN AUDIENCE
DEMOGRAPHICS TO U.S. 2000 CENSUS DATA

All statistically significant differences between subgroups are noted in the text, but this research doesn't show many. There are statistically significant differences in the Western population in terms of gender and age, as well as preferences among specific groups for John Wayne versus Clint Eastwood—but that's it. Although findings suggest some specific movies might be more popular among a particular subgroup (*The Searchers* among white men, for example), there are not enough people choosing any specific movie as a favorite to be able to determine if these differences are statistically significant.

APPENDIX B

The following is the text of the press release I sent to entertainment editors at over 600 newspapers around the country in 1994:

To: Entertainment Editor

RE: Press Release

An American popular culture researcher in Providence, Rhode Island, is investigating America's fascination with the movie Western. Stereotypically, the Western movie buff is a conservative white male whose love of John Wayne reflects politically incorrect attitudes of racism, sexism, and imperialism. But an informal survey has found that numbers of people from diverse backgrounds love Westerns for surprising reasons. One white housewife loves John Wayne because she can imagine herself free and independent. One Pawnee elder loves the Pawnee in *Dances with Wolves*, admiring young warriors who defend their land and die courageously. A black advertising executive has seen every Clint Eastwood Western, enjoying the notion that one man can succeed against all odds, embattled by a hostile and often corrupt society.

Westerns may not be for everybody, but if you love movie Westerns, if the sight of thundering hooves makes your heart race and you want to participate in this survey, write for a questionnaire to:

I LOVE WESTERNS
P.O. BOX 6051
PROVIDENCE, RI 02940

∩ ∩ ∩

Although the press release was designed to encourage participation from Western fans who did not fit the "stereotypic" profile (i.e., conservative white men), I had no control over how newspapers chose to run the item. For example, in July, *The Boston Herald* simply printed:

> I LOVE WESTERNS: If you love John Wayne and the sound of thundering hooves and want to be part of a national survey to find out what Americans' favorite Westerns are and why, write for a questionnaire to: I Love Westerns, [etc.].

I received nine completed questionnaires as a result of this item, six from white men, two from white women, and one from a black woman. Similarly, in July, *The Denver Post* ran:

> A researcher in American popular culture is studying America's fascination with the movie western. She wants to know more about the people who enjoy western films and what their favorites are. To participate in the study, write for a questionnaire to: I Love Westerns, [etc.].

In total, I received 33 completed questionnaires from the Denver area, nine from white men, 18 from white women, three from men of color, and three from women of color.

At least 45 newspapers carried word of the survey, inviting their readers to participate by writing to me for a questionnaire. There may have been more, but these are the publications respondents told me about:

Alexandria Daily Town Talk (LA)

Anchorage Daily News (AK)

Bangor Daily News (ME)

Beaumont Enterprise (TX)

Billings Gazette (MT)

Boston Herald (MA)

Capper's Weekly Newspaper (KS)

Casper Star Tribune (WY)

Clarion Ledger (Jackson, MS)

Denver Post (CO)

Delaware County Times (DE)

Fairbanks Daily News Miner (AK)

Florida Times Union (Jacksonville, FL)

Gazette Telegraph (Colorado Springs, CO)

George Street Journal (Providence, RI)

Idaho Statesman (Boise, ID)

In Newsweekly (Boston, MA)

Kansas City Film Society Newsletter (KS)

Kansas City Star (KS)

Lubbock Avalanche Journal (TX)

Miami Herald (FL)

Minnesota Star-Tribune (Minneapolis, MN)

Mobile Press Register (AL)

Montgomery County Journal (MD)

News Observer (Raleigh, NC)

Orange Leader (TX)

Pentagraph (IL)

Press of Atlantic City (NJ)

Providence Journal-Bulletin (RI)

Register Guard (Eugene, OR)

Roanoke Times & World News (VA)

Rockland Journal News (NY)

Rocky Mountain News (Denver, CO)

St. Paul Press (MN)

San Antonio Express-News (TX)

Sarasota Herald-Tribune (FL)

Setonian (Seton Hall University, NJ)

Sioux City Journal (IA)

Sun Herald (Biloxi-Gulfport, MS)

Sun Sentinel (Ft. Lauderdale, FL)

Union Tribune (San Diego, CA)

Virginian Pilot (Norfolk, VA)

Washington Sun (DC)

Winston-Salem Journal (NC)

Worcester Telegram (MA)

I Love Westerns Questionnaire

Gender: ___ M ___ F   Age: _____   Race/Ethnicity: _____

In what state did you spend your formative years, ages 3-16 (if outside the United States, what country)?

_____

Education: _____

Military Experience: _____

Occupation: _____

Estimated Household Annual Income:

    _____ $25,000 or below

    _____ $25,000—$49,999

    _____ $50,000—$74,999

    _____ $75,000—$99,999

    _____ $100,000 or above

Everyone feels strongly about certain social and political issues. What issues are important to you, and where do you stand on them?

_____
_____
_____
_____
_____

How did you hear of this survey? _____

Why do you love movie Westerns? What makes you say that?

_____
_____
_____
_____
_____

What is your *favorite* movie Western? _____

What makes it your favorite? What makes you say that?

_____
_____
_____
_____
_____
_____

When watching your favorite movie Western, what emotions do you experience? What about the movie or your life (past or present) do you think makes you have that emotional reaction?

_____
_____
_____
_____
_____

What would you say is the *best* movie Western ever made? _____

What makes it the best?_____

_____

_____

_____

_____

_____

If you would like to share your opinions and thoughts about Westerns with the author, copy this questionnaire, fill it out, and send it to:

MAVERICK SPIRIT PRESS
I LOVE WESTERNS SURVEY
P.O. BOX 113
MANVILLE, RI 02838

You can also take the survey online at *www.ilovewesterns.com/questionnaire*. Your comments may be used anonymously in future editions of this book.

If you would be willing to be contacted by the author for possible followup questions, please provide the following information:

Name_____ Phone # _____

Best time to be contacted_____

Street address_____

Email address_____

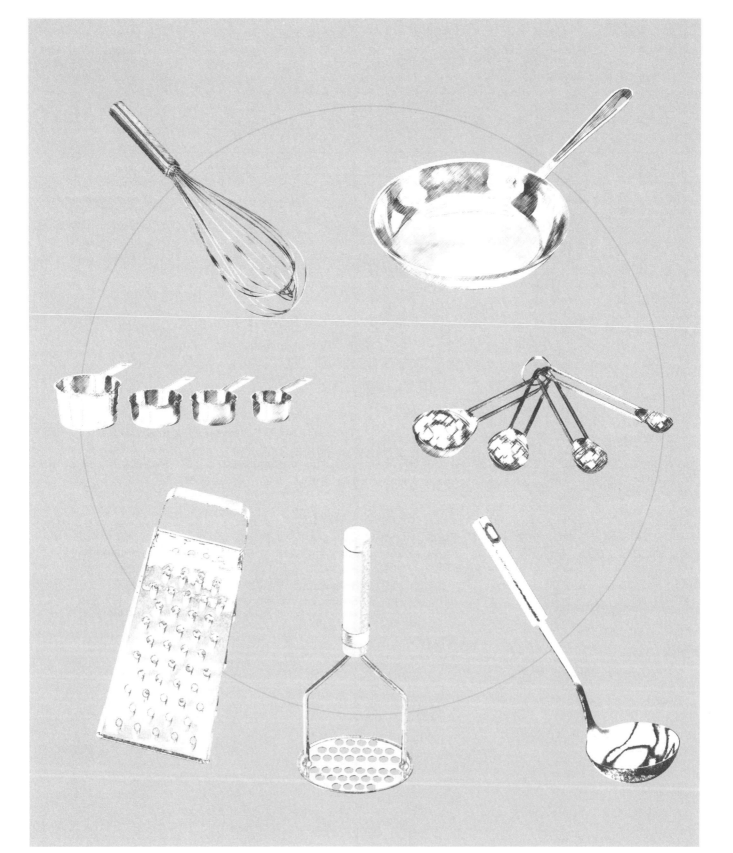

APPENDIX D

NEW SURVEY:

WHY WE LOVE COOKING SHOWS

What, you may ask, do cooking shows have to do with Westerns? Nothing…and everything. On the one hand, it is certainly a stretch to equate the two; sometimes food and travel shows feature Western style food or take you to chili/chuckwagon cookoff events, but the two are very different forms of popular entertainment. Westerns and cooking shows, however, are both cultural phenomena. They draw large and diverse audiences, appeal to deeply rooted values and sensibilities, and are hugely enjoyable for their fans.

Wild Open Spaces: Why We Love Westerns is the first in a series of books. *Why We Love Cooking Shows* is going to be the second. I would like to invite you to be part of the *Why We Love Cooking Shows* project by filling out this survey and having your opinions and experiences reflected in the book. Just why do we love cooking shows so much? What do they do for us? What are our favorites? What types of foods do we love to see prepared? Why do so many of us enjoy watching chefs prepare foods we would never prepare ourselves, maybe even never eat?

Home (NBC-TV, 1954), food editor Kit Kinne, courtesy Photofest

So if you love cooking shows, if the sizzle of a thick steak grilling over hot coals sets your mouth to watering, if the spectacle of a glitzy cooking competition leaves you gaping, or if watching a thick caramel sauce poured over a gooey chocolate dessert makes your eyes cross, complete the questionnaire on the next few pages and send it to:

MAVERICK SPIRIT PRESS
I LOVE COOKING SHOWS SURVEY
P.O. BOX 113
MANVILLE, RI 02838

You can also fill out the survey online at www.ilovecookingshows.com/questionnaire. Your responses may be used anonymously in the *Why We Love Cooking Shows* book. Let your voice be heard!

I Love Cooking Shows Questionnaire

Gender: ___ M ___ F   Age: _____   Race/Ethnicity: _____

In what state did you spend your formative years, ages 3-16 (if outside the United States, what country)?

_____

Education: _____

Military Experience: _____

Occupation: _____

Estimated Household Annual Income: ____ $25,000 or below

                                            ____ $50,000–$74,999

                                            ____ $75,000–$99,999

                                            ____ $100,000 or above

Everyone feels strongly about certain social and political issues. What issues are important to you, and where

do you stand on them?

_____

_____

_____

_____

_____

How did you hear of this survey? _____

What role does food play in your life/your family's life (aside from keeping you alive)? What makes you say that?

_____

_____

_____

_____

_____

_____

What is it about cooking shows that you love so much? What makes you say that?

_____

_____

_____

_____

_____

_____

What is your *favorite* cooking show (past or present)?

_____

What makes it your favorite? Please be specific.

_____

_____

_____

_____

_____

When watching your favorite cooking show, what emotions do you experience? What about the show or your life (past or present) do you think makes you have that emotional reaction?

_____

_____

_____

What type of food do you *most* like to see prepared? (This can be anything—whatever comes to mind for you.)

_____

_____

What makes it so enjoyable to watch that type of food being prepared?

_____

_____

_____

How often do you cook foods you have seen prepared on a cooking show? Why is that?

_____

_____

_____

Do you ever enjoy watching food prepared on a cooking show that you would never eat? If so, what makes that enjoyable?

_____

_____

_____

Can you give a specific example of enjoying watching a food prepared that you would never eat? What made it fun to watch?

_____

_____

_____

If you would like to share your opinions and thoughts about cooking shows with the author, copy this questionnaire, fill it out, and send it to:

MAVERICK SPIRIT PRESS
I LOVE COOKING SHOWS
P.O. BOX 113
MANVILLE, RI 02838

You can also take the survey online at _www.ilovecookingshows.com/questionnaire._
Your comments may be used anonymously in the book, _Why We Love Cooking Shows._

If you would be willing to be contacted by the author for possible follow-up questions, please provide the following information:

Name _____   Phone # _____

Best time to be contacted _____

Street address _____

Email address _____

BIBLIOGRAPHY

WESTERN FILMS

Blake, Michael. *Dances With Wolves*. New York: Fawcett Gold Medal, 1988.

Blake, Michael F. *Code of Honor: The Making of Three Great American Westerns*. New York: Taylor Trade Publishing, 2003.

Bogdanovich, Peter. *John Ford*. Berkeley: University of California Press, 1978.

Buscomb, Edward. *BFI Film Classics: The Searchers*. London: British Film Institute, 2000.

Buscomb, Edward, ed. *The BFI Companion to the Western*. New York: Atheneum, 1988.

Carey, Harry Jr. *Company of Heroes: My Life as an Actor in the John Ford Stock Company*. Metuchen, New Jersey: The Scarecrow Pres, Inc., 1994.

Cawelti, John G. *The Six-Gun Mystique Sequel*. Bowling Green, Ohio: Bowling Green State University Popular Press, 1999.

Churchill, Ward. *Fantasies of the Master Race: Literature, Cinema and the Colonization of American Indians*. Maine: Common Courage Press, 1992.

Harry Belafonte as The Preacher, *Buck and the Preacher* (1972), courtesy Photofest

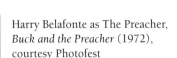

175

Countryman, Edward and Evonne von Heussen-Countryman. *BFI Film Classics: Shane*. London: British Film Institute, 1999.

Dortch, Joel. *Roy Rogers Biography*. *http://www.royrogers.com/roy_rogers_bio.html*.

Drummond, Phillip. *BFI Film Classics: High Noon*. London: British Film Institute, 1997.

Etulain, Richard W. and Glenda Riley. *The Hollywood West: Lives of Film Legends Who Shaped It*. Golden, Colorado: Fulcrum Publishing, 2001.

Eyles, Allen. *John Wayne*. New York: A.S. Barnes and Co., 1976.

Fenin, George N. and William K. Everson. *The Western: from silents to the seventies*. New York: Grossman Publishers, 1973.

Flynn, Peter. "The Silent Western as Mythmaker," *Images*, issue 6, Q2 2003, www.imagesjournal.com/issue06/infocus/western.htm.

Gallagher, Tag. *John Ford: The Man and His Films*. Berkeley: University of California Press, 1986.

Hardy, Phil. *The Western: The Complete Film Sourcebook*. New York: William Morrow and Company, Inc., 1983.

Holland, Ted. *B Western Encyclopedia: Facts, Photos and Filmographies for More than 250 Familiar Faces*. North Carolina: McFarland & Company, Inc., 1989.

Kael, Paulene. "Films in Review," *The New Yorker*, 25 Feb. 1974.

Kapsis, Robert E. and Kathie Coblentz, ed. *Clint Eastwood Interviews*. Jackson: University Press of Mississippi, 1999.

Kazanjian, Hoard and Chris Enss. *The Cowboy and the Senorita: A Biography of Roy Rogers and Dale Evans*. Guilford, Connecticut: Twodot, 2004.

Kilpatrick, Jacquelyn. *Celluloid Indians Native Americans and Film*. Lincoln: University of Nebraska Press, 1999.

Lenihan, John H. *Showdown: Confronting Modern America in the Western Film*. Chicago: University of Illinois Press, 1985.

Levy, Emanuel. *John Wayne: Prophet of the American Way of Life*. Metuchen: The Scarecrow Press, Inc., 1988.

McGhee, Richard D. *John Wayne: Actor, Artist, Hero*. Jefferson: McFarland and Company, Inc., Publishers, 1990.

Meyer, William R. *The Making of the Great Westerns*. New York: Arlington House Publishers, 1979.

Nachbar, Jack. "Horses, Harmony, Hope, and Hormones: Western Movies, 1930-1946," *Journal of the West*, Vol. 22, No. 4, October 1983.

Quirk, James R. *Photoplay*, April 1929.

Parks, Rita. *The Western Hero in Film and Television: Mass Media Mythology*. Ann Arbor: UMI Research Press, 1982.

Savage, William W. Savage, Jr. *The Cowboy Hero: His Image in American History and Culture*. Norman: University of Oklahoma Press, 1979.

Schickel, Richard. *Clint Eastwood: A Biography*. New York: Knopf Publishing Company, 1997.

Sinclair, Andrew. *John Ford: A Biography*. New York: Lorrimer Publishing, Inc., 1979.

Stedman, Raymond William. *Shadows of the Indian: Stereotypes in American Culture*. Norman: University of Oklahoma Press, 1982.

Slotkin, Richard. *Gunfighter Nation: The Myth of the Frontier in Twentieth-Century America*. New York: Atheneum, 1992.

Studlar, Gaylyn and Matthew Bernstein, ed. *John Ford Made Westerns: Filming the Legend in the Sound Era*. Bloomington: Indiana University Press, 2001.

Thoene, Bodie, and Rona Stuck. "Navajo Nation Meets Hollywood: An Inside Look at John Ford's Classic Westerns," *American West*. 5:20, Sept/Oct 1983.

Thompson, Douglas. *Clint Eastwood: Riding High*. NTC/Contemporary Publishing, 1993.

Tompkins, Jane. *West of Everything: The Inner Life of Westerns*. New York: Oxford University Press, 1992.

Tuska, Jon. *The American West in Film: Critical Approaches to the Western*. Connecticut: Greenwood Press, 1985.

Wills, Gary. *John Wayne's America*. New York: Touchstone, 1997.

WESTERN HISTORY

Billington, Ray Allen and Martin Ridge. *Westward Expansion: A History of the American Frontier*. New York: MacMillan Publishing Co., Inc., 1982.

Blaine, Martha Royce. *Pawnee Passage: 1870-1875*. Norman: University of Oklahoma Press, 1990.

Dary, David. *Cowboy Culture: A Saga of Five Centuries*. New York: Avon Books, 1981.

Deloria, Vine, Jr. *Custer Died for Your Sins: An Indian Manifesto*. Norman: University of Oklahoma Press, 1988.

Durham, Philip and Everett L. Jones. *The Negro Cowboys*. Lincoln: University of Nebraska Press, 1965.

Dykstra, Robert R. *The Cattle Towns*. New York: Atheneum, 1979.

Garrett, Greg. "The American West and the American Western: Printing the Legend," *Journal of American Culture*. Summer 1991, volume 14, number 2, pp. 99-105.

Grossman, James R, ed. *The Frontier in American Culture: Essays by Richard White and Patricia Nelson Limerick*. Berkeley: University of California Press, 1994.

Hine, Robert V. and John Mack Faragher. *The American West: A New Interpretive History*. New Haven: Yale University Press, 2000.

Katz, William Loren. *The Black West*. Seattle: Open Hand Publishing, Inc., 1987.

Limerick, Patricia Nelson. *The Legacy of Conquest: The Unbroken Past of the American West*. New York: W. W. Norton and Company, 1987.

McGrath, Roger D. *Gunfighters, Highwaymen, and Vigilantes: Violence on the Frontier*. Berkeley: University of California Press, 1987.

Payton, B.A., Gary Fiegehen, and Jim Skipp. *Cowboy: The Legend and the Legacy*. Vancouver: Greystone Books, 2000.

Rosa, Joseph G. *The Gunfighter: Man or Myth?* Norman: University of Oklahoma Press, 1969.

Rosa, Joseph G. and Robin May. *Buffalo Bill and His Wild West: A Pictorial Biography*. Lawrence: University Press of Kansas, 1989.

Russell, Don. *The Wild West: A History of the Wild West Shows*. Fort Worth, Texas: Amon Carter Museum of Western Art, 1970.

Weston, Jack. *The Real American Cowboy*. New York: Schocken Books, 1985.

White, Richard. *"It's Your Misfortune and None of My Own:" A New History of the American West*. Norman: University of Oklahoma Press, 1991.

INDEX

Page numbers in **bold type** refer to photographs.

Index to Fan Quotes

Page numbers refer to quotes and comments from survey respondents listed by occupation; ethnicity; and country, state, or region.

GET YOUR AUTOGRAPHED COPY

Yes, I want _____ copies of *Wild Open Spaces: Why We Love Westerns,* autographed by the author, at $24.95 each, plus $5 shipping for the first book and $2 for each additional book. (Rhode Island residents please add $1.75 sales tax per book.) Allow 15 days for delivery.

To place your order, you can:

Call 1-401-405-0178 with your credit card;

Fax this form with your credit card number to 1-401-633-6388;

Email your order with a credit card number to sales@maverickspiritpress.com;

Use our secure ordering at www.maverickspiritpress.com; or

Mail this form with a check or money order to Maverick Spirit Press, P.O. Box 113, Manville, RI 02838, USA

Name: _____

Address (no P.O. boxes, please): _____

City: _____ State: _____ Zip: _____

Telephone: _____ email address: _____

Payment:

☐ Check or money order enclosed

☐ Visa   ☐ MasterCard   ☐ AMEX   ☐ Discover

Card number: _____

Name on card: _____ Expiration date: _____

MUCH OBLIGED, PARDNER!

ADIOS !